THE
SIEGE OF
JERUSALEM

SELECTED WRITINGS OF
PAULINE ROSE

MESSIANIC
LUMINARIES
SERIES

THE
SIEGE OF
JERUSALEM

SELECTED WRITINGS OF
PAULINE ROSE

Compiled, Edited, and Revised
by Boaz Michael

VINE OF DAVID

VINE OF DAVID

The Siege of Jerusalem: Pauline Rose
Published 2016 by Vine of David, a publishing ministry of
First Fruits of Zion, Inc.

First Edition: 1949 Patmos Press, London
Second Edition: 1972 Old City Press, Jerusalem
Third Edition: 2016 Vine of David, Jerusalem

Design, editing, and compiling: Jerusalem, Israel
Printing and distribution: USA

Comments and questions may be sent to: feedback@vineofdavid.org

Vine of David is a publishing arm of the ministry of First Fruits of Zion dedicated to providing liturgical resources for the Messianic Jewish movement and to resurrecting the voices of Messianic pioneers and luminaries. If you would like to assist in the publication of these voices from the past, you can sponsor the translation and publication of their important works by visiting www.vineofdavid.org for needs and opportunities.

The Bram Center for Messianic Jewish Learning is in the heart of Jerusalem. Short term learning, day tours, or to visit The Bram Center please write to: info@thebramcenter.org.

Vine of David
Israel / United States / Canada

US Distribution: PO Box 649, Marshfield, Missouri 65706-0649 USA
Phone (417) 468-2741, www.ffoz.org

ISBN: 978-1-941534-16-8

Also available from Vine of David:
Window on Mount Zion
The Delitzsch Hebrew Gospels: A Hebrew / English Translation
Love and the Messianic Age
Love and the Messianic Age: Study Guide and Commentary
The Everlasting Jew

First Fruits of Zion: www.ffoz.org
Vine of David: www.vineofdavid.org

To Albert Rose

CONTENTS

ACKNOWLEDGEMENTS

Special thanks to Gershon Nerel and Paul Meier for sharing their archives and making the original articles available for this project. Thanks to the Jerusalem Foundation for maintaining Ha-Ohel and the Pauline Rose Garden. Thank you to Dr. Hagai Agmon-Snir director of the Jerusalem Intercultural Center. Thanks to Jacob Fronczak and Jordan Gayle Levy for translations from German and French respectively. Thanks to D. Thomas Lancaster for assembling the project, and compiling the research for the biography. Thanks to Miriam Lancaster for transcribing the articles and BBC audio. Thanks to Chris Moberg for help researching the Rose family. Thanks to Keren Pryor for her years of love and devotion to Pauline Rose and for sharing her story with so many. Thank you to the Vermeesch family for spending many precious hours of their time in Israel by assisting us in the quest for the Rose's gravesite and for helping us clean the gravestones. Thanks to the friends of Pauline Rose who shared their anecdotes and recollections. Thanks to the staff of First Fruits of Zion, Vine of David, and the Bram Center for reviving interest in Pauline Rose's writings. Thanks to the Mount Zion community for keeping the memory of Pauline Rose alive. Thank you to our *FFOZ Friends* for helping us resurrect the voices of early Messianic Judaism. Without their generosity, this book and others like it would not be financially feasible or at all possible.

INTRODUCTION TO
THE ORIGINAL EDITION

This book is compiled from notes from my diary and extracts from letters written during my stay in Jerusalem in the summer of 1946, and during the whole war period of 1948–1949.

It does not profess to be a comprehensive survey of the situation in Palestine and I have intentionally not dealt with the political, economic, and spiritual problems that contributed to this war.

I have only tried to give a few pictures of life as I experienced it in Jerusalem before, during, and after the siege.

As so many distorted pictures have been given to the world concerning the war in Palestine, this book is meant as a contribution to the truth regarding the unique and heroic stand of the Jewish people in the face of overwhelming odds.

Pauline Rose
JERUSALEM, JUNE, 1949.

INTRODUCTION TO
THE NEW EDITION

It has been seventy years since Pauline Rose first set foot in Palestine (summer of 1946), and the time has come for a fresh edition of her book *The Siege of Jerusalem*. This new edition includes articles and writings by the same author, which provide broader context for her story, explain her mission to Palestine, and create an appropriate epilogue to the drama. In her original version of the book, Pauline Rose "tried to give a few pictures of life" as she "experienced it in Jerusalem before, during, and after the siege." In that same spirit, the current edition attempts to offer more pictures of her life and insights before, during, and after Israel's War of Independence and the creation of the Jewish state. The additional material focuses especially on Pauline Rose's mission to establish Messianic Judaism in Israel.

The original edition of *The Siege of Jerusalem* appeared in 1949 under Messianic Jewish pioneer Abram Poljak's publisher PATMOS (17 Higham Road, Tottenham, England). Likewise, the additional writings of Pauline Rose appearing in this new edition originally appeared in various periodicals and books produced by Poljak and Patmos Press. Rose wrote for Poljak's mission journal *Jerusalem* (which appeared in both English and French editions) and *Die Judenchristliche Gemeinde* (a German language periodical).

Before republishing this work, First Fruits of Zion and Vine of David made exhaustive but ultimately unsuccessful efforts to find heirs, family members, or estate holders who might have some interest in the work or grant permission for the republication of Pauline Rose's writings. Albert and Pauline left behind no heirs, and their estate seems to have passed to the Jerusalem Foundation. In any case, from its inception, Patmos Press explicitly waived all copyright to all of its publications, granting blanket permission for the republication of works published under their imprint.

Pauline Rose's second book, *Window on Mount Zion*, tells the story of the house and garden she and her husband established on Mount Zion and their experiences there before, during, and after the Six-Day War. Pauline Rose narrated the same story in summary form in a BBC Radio 4 interview with Evie Garratt, which aired on August 13, 1968. Excerpts from that interview form the final chapter of this new edition of *The Siege of Jerusalem*.

In Pauline Rose's day, the term Messianic Judaism had not yet emerged into popular parlance, and up until the 1960s, Patmos Press used the term Jewish Christianity to communicate the concept. They later adopted the new terminology. To update the language in keeping with modern Messianic Jewish preferences, we have taken the liberty of changing the term "Jewish Christian" to "Messianic Judaism," "Messianic Jew," or "Messianic Jewish" as the case may dictate. Likewise, we have replaced the anglicized name "Jesus" with the Hebrew "Yeshua" and the title "Christ" with the Hebraic title "Messiah" when appropriate to do so.

As so many distorted pictures have been given to the world concerning the origins of Messianic Judaism, this book is meant as a contribution to the truth regarding the unique and heroic stand of Messianic Jews in the face of overwhelming odds.

Boaz Michael
JERUSALEM, ISRAEL
JUNE, 2016 | IYYAR 12, 5776

PSALM 124

A Song of Ascents. Of David.

If it had not been the LORD who was on our side—
    let Israel now say—
if it had not been the LORD who was on our side
    when people rose up against us,
then they would have swallowed us up alive,
    when their anger was kindled against us;
then the flood would have swept us away,
    the torrent would have gone over us;
then over us would have gone
    the raging waters.
Blessed be the LORD,
    who has not given us
    as prey to their teeth!
We have escaped like a bird
    from the snare of the fowlers;
the snare is broken,
    and we have escaped!
Our help is in the name of the LORD,
    who made heaven and earth.

THE LADY OF MOUNT ZION

THE PAULINE ROSE STORY
BOAZ MICHAEL

Pauline Rose (1898–1973) was called the "Lady of Mount Zion." She could also be considered the first lady of twentieth-century Messianic Judaism. Those who knew her speak of a woman of poise, cultured sophistication, and natural grace. In a 1969 BBC radio interview, Evie Garratt described her as "a serenely beautiful woman with a scarcely lined face topped by a crown of silver hair." The epitaph on her grave stone eulogizes her with the words from *Eishet Chayil*, "Many daughters have done nobly, but you excel them all" (Proverbs 31:29). The story of her intersection with Messianic Judaism and the modern State of Israel grants her a celebrity status in the Messianic Jewish movement.

Pauline reveals little about her own personal story prior to her involvement in Messianic Judaism and her work in Israel. She was born into a Jewish family in Johannesberg, South Africa, on Erev Shabbat, September 2, 1898, (Elul 15, 5659). Her tombstone provides her father's name (Rabbi Sha'ul Robinson) and her Jewish name Pesyah. She had at least one sister. She filled her early years with a variety of pursuits ranging from piano playing to watercolour painting and professional dressmaking. At some point in her youth, she met Albert Rose and they were married.

Albert (Azriel) Rose (1883–1977) was born on August 30, 1883 (Av 27, 5643) in Lithuania to Meyer and Golda Rose in Shavl (Šiauliai). The Rose family immigrated to South Africa in 1890 and settled in Oudtshoorn, Cape Province, the ostrich capital of the world. Albert and his older brother Max became ostrich farmers and they made their fortune in the ostrich feather industry at a time when ostrich plumage was all the rage in high fashion. Albert and Max were among the most successful feather suppliers in the country, and they had a reputation as the "ostrich feather kings" of South Africa.[1] The demand for ostrich feathers declined in 1914 with the outbreak of World War I, and ostrich plumes were, thereafter, no longer considered fashionable. With the collapse of the feather market, the Rose fortunes began to dwindle.

Pauline and Albert were married sometime during the ostrich years. Albert was fifteen years her senior. Albert and Pauline had one son together, but the boy died young. Trauma over that bereavement sent Pauline on a quest for meaning. She spent her days searching through various philosophies and teachings, but nothing satisfied her. She wrote, "For many years, I questioned the existence of God, and the meaning of my life, or of life on earth altogether. What did it matter? … I waded through the religious teachings of East and West … I made a search through philosophies old and new."

Pauline's quest for truth eventually brought her to the conviction of God's existence. She said, "If there was a guiding power and a law governing the smallest flower on earth, there must be a guiding power for me also." She began to seek that guiding power.

In 1931, Albert and Pauline left both the ostrich business and South Africa. Albert's brother Max chose to remain in Oudtshoorn. He kept his ostriches despite the decline, hoping for a resurgence in the market.[2]

---

[1] David Zetler, "The Ostrich King," Jerusalem Post (1/25/2007), online at www.jpost.com/Magazine/Features/The-ostrich-king.

[2] Joan Comay, Lavinia Cohn-Sherbok, "Rose, Max" in *Who's Who in Jewish History: After the Period of the Old Testament*, (Routledge; Taylor & Francis Books Ltd; Reprint Edition: Florence, KY, 1995) 317–318.

Albert found work in London and became a successful builder and property developer. He was instrumental in building most of the houses in the NW2/NW10 area of London in the 1930s.[3] Pauline became a designer for one of the great fashion houses in Paris. Meanwhile, Pauline's quest for truth continued. She found some solace, peace, and freedom in artistic expression, and she expressed her faith in God through painting "in an endeavour to produce the beauty which is born of the perfect harmony of line, form and colour, welded together by that mysterious power."

Ultimately, however, aesthetic expression was not enough, and Pauline continued her quest for truth. She joined a theosophical religious community that valued communal living, sharing all things in common, while concentrating on developing personal spirituality manifested in brotherly love. The group studied all religions and accepted all religions, and they conducted daily readings from the great religious texts of the world's religions. In this way, Pauline became more familiar with the Bible. In the Bible she started to find the type of revelation she sought. In the Tanach she found a bedrock of faith in God and came to understand the mission of her own Jewish people, but she did not look for truth in the New Testament:

> I had been told that all light on the Jewish way was held within the pages of the Old Testament. The New Testament was not the word of God spoken to the Jews. It was a Gentile religion.

The seemingly idyllic world of religious tolerance and philosophical meditation into which she had entered, however, had a dark underside of occultism. Pauline Rose encountered some type of Spiritism in that context and seems to have come away frightened and disturbed by the incident. She said, "I was lured into my first experience of actual contact with the spiritual forces, both good and bad, that hide behind the screen of loftiest ideals.

---

3   Personal communication with a 1975 visitor to Ha-Ohel.

Innocently I walked into unknown dangers; wiser and more enlightened I emerged."

In 1936, the Roses visited Germany, seeking family members displaced by the Nazis. Pauline recounted, "I came to look for my relatives who were among the first of Hitler's victims. Some I found in hiding, others disappeared without leaving a trace behind." Firsthand experience with Nazi Germany made a strong impact on her. She said, "I was filled with horror, fear, and shame, and a helplessness that led to despair. I left Germany vowing within myself that I would never again set foot in the country, nor have contact with anything or anyone connected with it."

Over the course of the war, the Roses lost family members in the death camps. In 1945, a relative originally from South Africa arrived in London to stay with Roses. She had survived the Warsaw Ghetto, the horrors of the death camps, and the final death march. Her stories of suffering and human misery made a profound impact on the Roses.

The Roses themselves prospered during World War II through the development of a farm outside of London. Before the outbreak of the war, Albert and Pauline purchased a large tract of land originally intended as property for a building site. Pauline referred to it as "a peaceful oasis of green cultivated land." The Roses took residence in a cottage on the property. During the war, the British government wanted the land utilized for agriculture. The Roses took over the management of the estate and cultivated it. Their farm became famous for its exotic vegetables, fruits, and flowers, some grown in England for the first time. The Roses introduced agricultural innovations that had not been seen in England previously. For example, the Roses developed underground heating to grow crops in the winter, and they introduced commercial production of both corn and eggplant. Their property became the famous Heston Farm outside of London.

At some point before or during World War II, Pauline Rose's quest for truth led her to some type of encounter with Yeshua of Nazareth, but she seems to have received and understood him in Jewish terms:

Then, in my despair, Yeshua revealed himself to me. From one moment to the next I was transported from the depths of despair to the heights of joy. From that time the Spirit began the work of transformation within me and I saw Yeshua not only as my personal Saviour, but also as the Messiah of Israel.

Pauline Rose's encounter with the New Testament and Yeshua of Nazareth left her transformed, and she found herself taking up the yoke of discipleship and following after the man from Nazareth:

It was as though one veil after another was lifted from my eyes; one door after another was opened, until I walked on and on into eternity, the torchbearer of eternal life guiding me step by step.

We do not know the details of how Pauline Rose first encountered Yeshua or how it was that he revealed himself to her. Did she have contact with Christian missionaries or a denomination group? Was she ever baptised into a church, or did she come to her conclusions about the Jewishness of Yeshua from the outset? If she ever did spend some time as a member of a conventional church, it did not seem to leave a theological mark on her. Pauline's devotion to Yeshua did not compromise her own sense of Jewish identity or diminish her allegiance to Judaism. The Jesus she found in the New Testament was the Jewish Yeshua who did not come to abolish the Torah. If anything, her devotion to Yeshua of Nazareth compelled her to become a better Jew. One Jewish friend who knew her personally relates, "She wanted to let her beliefs animate her Jewish life without advertising it."

Pauline Rose's newfound devotion to Yeshua did not persuade her husband. Albert remained a devoutly observant, traditionalist Jew all his life, and he never identified himself with his wife's new Messiah. At the same time, it does not appear that he ever tried to discourage her enthusiasm or dissuade her, nor did she make her faith a point of contention with him.

In 1944, Pauline Rose encountered Messianic Jewish pioneer Abram Poljak and his small Messianic community in London. Abram Poljak had only recently been released from an internment camp in Canada where he had spent most of the war. Prior to the war, Poljak had rallied together Jewish Christians under the banner of the cross in the star of David. He had worked closely with Messianic pioneer Paul Philip Levertoff to form a Jewish Christian Union, and he had campaigned to establish Messianic Jewish communities in Europe and Israel. He was most famous for a book by the name of *The Cross in the Star of David*. At the time of his release from internment, Poljak returned to London and re-established his Messianic Jewish work in the midst of the Nazi blitz. Unperturbed by air raid sirens and bombs, Poljak's small Sabbath fellowship met on Friday nights in a humble room on the top of a tenement house in the East End of London to kindle "the Sabbath Light of Messiah," to say Kiddush, and to welcome the Sabbath in honour of Yeshua the Messiah. In the summer of 1944, Pauline Rose found her way into Poljak's community and into Messianic Judaism:

> It was to one of these Friday evening services that I was guided, and the sincere spirit of truth and love that I found in that small gathering showed me that my search for a spiritual home was ended. I had found brethren with whom I was to work from then on in a common spiritual calling.

Rose became an active member of the community and an eager learner. At first, she was amused by the community's seemingly grandiose aspirations to become "a worldwide movement," but as she began to understand the vision of Messianic Judaism and the kingdom of heaven, she became a devoted advocate for the community's goals, and she marched with them under their flag of "the Cross in the Star of David."

Poljak's group focused on eschatology and particularly the coming kingdom of heaven. Expectation of a literal Messianic Era on earth ignited Pauline Rose's faith, and she found confidence in that future hope. She believed that the formation of the Jewish State in Palestine was an indication of the nearness of the coming of Messiah and the establishment of the kingdom.

At the end of 1945, Pauline received a letter from her sister, who was visiting Palestine, inviting her to come and meet her there. On March 18, 1946, Pauline made her first trip to the land. She considered herself to be on a mission from God to bring Messianic Judaism into Palestine. She said, "The time had come for the Sabbath light of the Messiah to be kindled in the Holy Land." For four months she met with Christians and Messianic Jews, seeking kindred spirits who shared Poljak's vision for establishing a Messianic Jewish synagogue. The experience discouraged and fatigued her. She met with strong resistance. The believers she encountered warned her that any association with Judaism or the Jewish people would lead her to destruction. She felt assaulted by the powers of darkness in a spiritual battle:

> Here I met Jews who rejected the wisdom of the Bible; who were proud in their own wisdom. There were those who followed the law to the last letter, knowing nothing of its true spirit. There were also others who accepted the Word of God and believed in His salvation—waiting for the Messiah, knowing that only He could redeem them.
>
> Here I met also Gentiles representing the many different ways of the Christian churches. Each one with a variant doctrine, a point of dispute, concerning the interpretation of the Bible. I met those of different sects who had grown up outside the churches; each one believing they had a special truth revealed to them, and insisting that all others accept that truth.
>
> I saw amongst the Jews the same situation that existed at the same time of Moses, and at the time of Yeshua. The same willfulness, the same wickedness, the same blindness. I saw amongst the Gentiles the self-righteousness and hypocrisy, the anti-Semitism that had developed

with the growth of the churches away from the true spirit of Christianity.[4]

Despite the spiritual resistance and her own disillusionment, Rose managed to assemble a small congregation of ten brothers and sisters in the Master to kindle Sabbath candles and welcome the Sabbath in Jerusalem:

> On June 22, 1946, in a small room in an Arab house, I kindled the Sabbath light of the Messiah for the first time in Jerusalem. This date marks the foundation of the synagogue of the Messiah in the Holy City.

The next Sabbath, however, the political situation changed, and the British imposed a strict curfew on the Jews of Jerusalem. Rose took advantage of a last minute flight and returned to England.

Pauline Rose's second trip to Palestine came after the UN's decision to partition. Pauline wanted to be back in Jerusalem, continuing the work she had pioneered the previous year. She arrived in Palestine on February 11, 1948, and eventually made her way to Jerusalem by armoured car on March 8, where she found herself trapped in the midst of the siege, unable to leave the city, suffering the same deprivations and dangers as the rest of the people:

> There were fears and doubts, bullets, shells, and all the influences of war. However, the light was kindled every Sabbath eve, and the people of the Sabbath and the power of the light of the Messiah brought comfort and strengthening to the Community and all its friends. The light of the Messiah shone brightly in Israel—in Jerusalem, even during its starkest days.

---

[4] Pauline Rose, "Hear O Israel," *Jerusalem: Organ of the Jewish Christian Community and the Jerusalem Fellowship*, 39 (December, 1949). This description of her first trip to Palestine appears near the end of the original article.

The contents of Pauline Rose's first book, *Siege of Jerusalem*, describe her adventures in the war zone and detail the drama of enduring the siege, and the relief when supplies finally came into the city by way of the Burma Road. Abram Poljak provides another perspective on the story as he summarizes Pauline Rose's work for the Messianic Jewish community in Jerusalem during those tense months:

> Several times each day, Pauline Rose went through the rain of bullets from her flat in Rehaviah, a suburb, to our meeting place in the center of the New City of Jerusalem—often the only person to be seen in the streets. She also fetched food and water for other people who dared not go into the street; she assisted sick women in their housework and nursed patients in a hospital. Her faith and quiet heroism made her a shining example, keeping the Community together. The fact that, as a woman, she thus despised death carried the others along with her, and during all these months not one of the appointed services was canceled.[5]

Poljak also tells the story of how, after the siege of Jerusalem, the Stern Gang abducted Pauline Rose and four other leaders of the Messianic Jewish community in August 1948. The terrorists became suspicious of Pauline Rose because she held a British passport, spoke English, and, in Poljak's words, "looks like a Gentile." The Stern Gang members believed that she was a British spy and that the Messianic Jewish community in Jerusalem was a façade for British agents. The Stern Gang had a reputation for shooting people they believed to be spies. The terrorists interrogated, threatened, and terrorized the five disciples. Under coercion and threats, one woman denied her faith in Yeshua, promising the Sternists that she would have nothing more to do with the community. She

---

[5]   Abram Poljak, "Letters from Mount Carmel," *The Jewish Christian Community* 28 (January 1949).

was released, but Pauline Rose and the other three community members remained in the custody of the Sternists.

Rose and her fellow community leaders did as the apostles of old and sang songs of praise in prison and witnessed to the light of the Messiah before the powers of darkness. They did not know if they would be released or shot to death.

Meanwhile the "arrest of the Jewish Christian Community" had become known in Jerusalem (a Hebrew daily paper reported about it), well-known Jews who knew Pauline Rose took up the case, convincing the Sternists that their accusations were untenable, and achieving the discharge of all.[6]

After their release, the leadership of the Jerusalem community expressed a desire to distance themselves from some of the overt Christian symbolism employed by Poljak (such as the cross in the Star of David) in favor of more neutral, Jewish iconography. Some of the leaders also objected to prayers addressed directly to Yeshua, and they insisted on praying to God in Yeshua's name. Some community members questioned conventional interpretations about Paul's teachings regarding the Law. They declared themselves the "New Community." In all of these measures, the New Community only anticipated what would later become normative in Messianic Judaism, but to Poljak, it seemed that the community had fallen into apostasy.

Poljak brought a swift and decisive correction. Pauline Rose and three of her co-leaders returned at once to the "Old Community," but on a subsequent conversation with Poljak, they restated their differences in perspective. Nevertheless, Pauline Rose suffered no censure from Poljak. Despite their differences, he did not consider her a schismatic or an apostate.

Gershon Nerel briefly summarizes the story of the theological upheaval in the Jerusalem fellowship in an article titled "A 'Messianic Jewish Church' in Eretz-Israel."[7] Federico Dal Bo's paper "The Theological and Cultural Challenge of Messianic Jews.

---

[6] Ibid.

[7] Gershon Nerel, "A 'Messianic Jewish Church' in Eretz-Israel?', *Mishkan* 29 (1998), 46, full articles 44–58

Towards a New Jewish Paradigm?" misconstrues Nerel's article and makes several inaccurate statements. He states that Pauline Rose (whom he also misidentifies as the wife of Abram Poljak) led a congregation called Jerusalem Jewish Christian Fellowship which "progressively moved to more liberal doctrinal tendencies, such as the rejection of the second coming of Jesus."[8] Dal Bo came to that conclusion from a misreading of Nerel's summary of the story; if he had consulted the primary sources, he would have found that Rose's convictions on Yeshua did not waiver. Instead, Pauline Rose continued to work with Abram Poljak and his Messianic Jewish community for many years, representing his work at conferences, writing for his journals, and boldly stating her faith. Despite speculation to the contrary, there is no indication that Pauline Rose ever hesitated in her faith or in her allegiance to Yeshua at that time or any time thereafter.

An anonymous Israeli believer in Yeshua who lived near the Roses and assisted them in their home on Mount Zion from 1968–1972 (almost until the year Pauline died) reported that she still remained constant in her hope in Yeshua, in the second coming, and in the advent of the Messianic Era. As a weekly Sabbath guest in the Rose home, the anonymous Israeli had a firsthand look into Albert and Pauline's faith and practice, which he described as "Orthodox Jewish—not fanatical, just Jewish." Moreover, he participated with Pauline in a ceremony that she conducted every Friday night, prior to the lighting the Sabbath candles. It was her custom, he said, to light a multi-branched menorah (apparently a seven-branched menorah) as a representation of "the Sabbath

---

[8] Federico Dal Bo, "The Theological and Cultural Challenge of Messianic Jews. Towards a New Jewish Paradigm?" *Pardes* 21 (2015), 49, full article 34–58

light of Messiah," which will shine in the kingdom.[9] Pauline Rose apparently inherited this unique ceremony from Abram Poljak's community, and Rose apparently propagated the ritual in the community she helped pioneer in Jerusalem. At the end of her life, she was still about the business of kindling the Sabbath light of Messiah.

After the conclusion of the War for Independence, Pauline returned to London where she remained active in the London community. She also travelled to Europe to speak in conferences about Messianic Judaism and the community in Jerusalem. Despite vowing never to set foot on German soil again, she returned to Germany in 1953 with a message of reconciliation and redemption for the German people.

In February of that same year, she also returned to Jerusalem and reconnected with the community she had planted. Pauline spent several months in Israel every year thereafter until, in 1959, she and Albert sold Heston Farm and made Israel their permanent home.[10] The story of how she and Albert acquired a house on Mount Zion, planted a garden there, and took a front row seat for the Six-Day War and the liberation of Jerusalem, is fully told in her second book, *Window on Mount Zion*.

Shortly after the Roses settled permanently in Jerusalem, a friend who had known them from the Heston Farm days asked Pauline, "Why don't you create a garden on Mount Zion?" This simple comment ignited a flame of faith within Pauline. She had always considered the Jewish return to the Holy Land and the

---

9 Personal interview with an elderly crypto-Messianic Israeli who prefers to keep his identity anonymous. The interview took place in May of 2016 in the outskirts of Jerusalem. This gentleman lived on Mount Zion in a home near and provided by the Roses. He and his wife (and some others who were part of a community on Mount Zion) assisted the Roses with guests, the garden, daily responsibilities, and were in their home for Sabbath gatherings each week. This interview was a gift from HaShem as it gave us a personal and first-hand account of Albert's and Pauline's life and filled in many remaining details of her time on Mount Zion.

10 Ann Carroll, "Faith Made It Possible" and "Pauline Rose Found Light in Bible," *El Paso Herald-Post* (April 3–4, 1974).

formation of the Jewish state to be a first flowering of the redemption. She reminded herself of the prophecy from Isaiah:

> Indeed, the LORD will comfort Zion; He will comfort all her waste places. And her wilderness He will make like Eden, and her desert like the garden of the LORD; joy and gladness will be found in her, thanksgiving and sound of a melody. (Isaiah 51:3)

What place was more deserted and left to waste than the torn war-zone of Mount Zion? Pauline came to the conviction that she and Albert needed to take a home on Mount Zion and plant a garden there in anticipation of the blossoming forth of the redemption. She knew that the LORD had promised to restore Zion. Now she wanted to participate in the fulfilment of those prophecies by taking part in that restoration. She wanted to find a house with a plot of land on desolate Mount Zion and make it bloom.

To everyone other than Pauline and Albert, the idea seemed absurd. Ever since the end of the War for Independence, Old City Jerusalem remained under the control of the Jordanian government. Jews had been banished from the city. Mount Zion was a militarized zone, right on the border between Israel and the Jordanians. No one lived on Mount Zion. The houses had been abandoned since the war, most of them derelict or reduced to rubble. Only the Israeli army occupied the hill, just opposite the Jordanian positions.

Nevertheless, Pauline and Albert, both up in years by then, persisted in faith. They ardently believed that the city would soon be restored and Zion would blossom. They prevailed upon the government to allow them to restore one of the homes on Mount Zion, but the matter was complicated by uncertainty over the status of those homes. After several years of persistent appeals, by some miracle, the authorities relented and gave the Roses their dream in the form of permission to occupy an abandoned two-story Jerusalem home near the Tomb of David and Zion Gate, a home only to pigeons and within the gun sights of the Jordanian soldiers.

The Roses transformed the pigeon house into a beautiful home of Jerusalem stone, tiled floors, and arched ceilings. They cultivated a lush English-styled flower garden, planted with exotic species from around the world. The house and the garden were physical expressions of Pauline's spiritual hopes. The Roses named the house "Ha-Ohel," that is, "The Tent," in memory of Abraham's tent, which was always open to guests, and in reference to the Tent of Meeting. They modelled their home after Abraham's legendary hospitality. Ha-Ohel became a meeting place for visitors to Mount Zion. Soldiers, Jews, Christians, Arabs, pilgrims of all faiths, artists, poets, thinkers, philosophers, and statesmen were all welcomed for tea in Ha-Ohel. The Roses dedicated the home to the universal ideals of peace and brotherhood that Jerusalem of the Messianic Era represents. Their home became a symbol of peace between all men, and in that home, they encouraged dialogue and mutual understanding between Jews, Christians, and Muslims alike.

The Roses served afternoon tea on a daily basis, and they had guests at their Sabbath table every Friday night. Conversations turned naturally to faith, prophecy, and the ultimate hope of humanity. In those days, Pauline Rose became known as "the Lady of Mount Zion."

Ironically, the location of the Rose house was only a stone's throw from the traditional location of the Tomb of David and the Upper Room (the Cenacle) which, according to Bargil Pixner, marks the location of an early Messianic Jewish place of assembly. After the destruction of Jerusalem in 70 CE, the original Jewish Yeshua community returned from Pella to rebuild in the ruins of the city. They felt compelled to rebuild on that same location and re-establish their presence there. Some archaeologists believe that they built a Messianic Jewish synagogue.[11] Some of its stones still stand today in the lower courses of the Cenacle. They assembled those stones from the rubble of the city in anticipation of the ultimate redemption of Zion. Pauline Rose probably did not know that the home she and Albert selected was in nearly the same location that the returning Jewish believers selected in 73 CE to express their own hope in prophecies of Zion's redemption.

Pauline Rose saw her hope in those prophecies vindicated in 1968. When the Six-Day War broke out, the Rose house was quite literally in the middle of the fight. Gunshots, machine gun fire, and explosions enveloped the home. As the Israeli army prepared to enter the Old City, an officer and his men stopped at Ha-Ohel for coffee before the assault. The officer lamented that they had no flag to carry with them on such a historically significant occasion. Pauline Rose dashed upstairs and returned with a white bed sheet. She produced a can of blue paint and painted a huge Star of David on the sheet. She took a stick from her garden to serve as a flagpole. The soldiers carried Pauline's flag into the battle, and when they conquered the Old City, they hoisted that same flag atop the Tower of David.

After the conquest of Jerusalem, Pauline and Albert were among the first Jews of Jerusalem to be able to pray at the Kotel (the Western Wall). In the ensuing days, as rivers of Israelis streamed to the holy place, making the ascent up Mount Zion, the Roses were there to welcome them back to the holy city of Jerusalem.

According to a personal friend of the Roses who knew them near the end of Pauline's life, Pauline was diagnosed with a form of lymphatic cancer in 1973, and she died shortly after receiving the diagnosis. Pauline Rose passed into the world of truth on

---

11   Bargil Pixner, "Church of the Apostles Found on Mount Zion," *Biblical Archaeology Review* 16:2 (May/June 1990): 17–35, 60. Cf. Bellarmino Bagatti, *The Church from the Circumcision* (Jerusalem, Israel: Franciscan Press, 1984), 125; D. Thomas Lancaster, "New Zion," *Torah Club: Chronicles of the Apostles* (Marshfield, MO; Jerusalem: First Fruits of Zion; 2016), 1221–1245.

September 20 (Elul 23, 5733)[12] of that year, two weeks and a few days before the outbreak of the Yom Kippur War. Albert lived on after her passing, and he remained at her home. He was still receiving guests from around the world at Ha-Ohel at least as late as 1975. He died on August 13, 1977 (Av 29, 5737). The inscriptions on the grave stones[13] of the Roses identify them as coming "From Mount Zion."

The Pauline Rose story is a tale of a woman of faith, a Messianic Jewish pioneer and luminary who possessed the power of far-reaching vision. The prophetic vision of the coming Messianic Age inspired her and drove her to plant and nurture the idea of Messianic Judaism for the last three decades of her life. Her story testifies to faith in a renewed and restored Jerusalem and the dawning of redemption, but the things that made Pauline truly remarkable were not her great faith or her prophetic insights, but rather, the simple, eloquent ways in which she expressed her faith in those prophecies: She lit candles in honor of Messiah on Friday nights, she planted a garden on Mount Zion in anticipation of the redemption, and she invited guests into her home for afternoon tea and Sabbath meals. To this day, her garden on Mount Zion still blooms in the hope of the coming King.

---

[12] In Judaism everything has meaning. It is no coincidence that Pauline was born and died in the Hebrew month of Elul. The Hebrew for Elul (אלול) forms an acronym for the phrase *ani l'dodi v'dodi li*, which means, "I am to my beloved and my beloved is to me." These romantic words from Solomon's Song of Songs speak of our relationship to the Creator, a relationship compared to that of a bride and groom. Pauline Rose's life, which began in Elul and ended in Elul, offers us a brief glimpse into a life of romance lived in close relationship with God.

[13] After months of searching we had the blessing of finding Pauline's and Albert's grave sites in Jerusalem. We were the first people to visit them in many years. With honor, we placed stones upon their graves indicating our respectful presence. We were blessed with the mitzvah of cleaning their weather-warn headstones. Upon completion, it was a special moment as we stood and considered their lives, spoke of Pauline's testimony, and said the appropriate prayers. We lit a candle and left red roses on her grave.

PART I
THE MISSION

CHAPTER ONE

HEAR, O ISRAEL

You said to me, dear friend, "How lucky are you to have such faith in God! How I envy your belief that you have a mission in life! I wish I could believe with you that the Jewish nation has a special mission in the world."[14]

FAITH IN GOD

Shall I tell you how I came to have such faith and such beliefs?

For many years I questioned the existence of God, and the meaning of my life, or of life on earth altogether. What did it matter what happened to me, or what I did—some good things, some bad things, some profitable, some useless? What was the purpose of my life? What was I here for? Why were there different races, different nations, different religions? Why was there so much destruction, unhappiness, struggle, and strife? There seemed to be no answer, no explanation, no reason in it at all.

But I became conscious that behind all the chaos and turmoil of human affairs there was an immutable law and order governing the universe. The laws of nature, the laws of destiny, the laws by which we were created. If there are laws, there must be a law-giver; if there is creation their must be a Creator.

---

[14] The following article contains answers to questions put to the author by many Jews in Jerusalem. It is not meant to be systematic or complete; rather does it show a way of thinking as a stimulus for the enquirer's own search and studies in the Scriptures. Jerusalem, 1949

I began to believe in God. He was hidden behind a cloud, but he existed. When the sun is covered by a cloud, there is still light on the earth—light from the hidden sun.

However small and unimportant I may be, I was created by the Creator of the universe, and therefore I must be on the earth for some purpose. For surely the Creator of heaven and earth, the giver of law and director of all life, would not put millions of human beings onto this earth without a reason and a purpose.

If there was a guiding power and a law governing the smallest flower on earth, there must be a guiding power for me also. I began to look for that guiding power in my life. At first it was very difficult, for I was used to depending upon my own will and reasoning power to direct my life. Most times there was a sharp clash between my will and the will of my Creator, but over and over again I saw that a power greater than my will made plans for me which cancelled my own plans and proved ultimately to be of the greatest wisdom and blessing for me, in spite of my rebellion and inability to understand.

In that way, dear friend, began my life in faith in God.

QUEST FOR TRUTH

With the recognition of a guiding power in my own personal life establishing my faith in God, I became identified with life as a whole. I wanted to find peace, harmony and beauty in my own life, believing that if I found them for myself, I could help others to find them too. The basic principal applying to my life was the same as for the whole of humanity.

I set out to find more light, and more understanding of the laws of God, which were intended to govern and guide human life, and produce peace, joy, and beauty.

I waded through religious teachings of East and West, which answered my questions by means of my heart and emotions. I made a search through philosophies, old and new, and found answers that calmed the rebellion of reason.

After much searching, reading, thinking, I became confused; I could not get a clear picture of the way to obtain a better life, and peace and joy on earth. Whenever I set out to control my life according to the "order" that I was seeking, there were interferences that changed the plan.

Then I reached the point where I believed that only through some form of creative art, a way of expressing all that I felt about life, could I find peace in myself and be of use to the world. I concentrated on painting in an endeavour to produce the beauty that is born of the perfect harmony of line, form, and colour, welded together by that mysterious power called "inspiration."

Through all this long journey in search of the way, the guiding power in my life became more and more apparent, and my faith increased in strength. My will became less rebellious and I was more willing to follow the guidance that so often rooted me out of the nice little "niche" I had made for myself, or ruthlessly opposed my own plan for my life.

It was a good thing to express what one felt about God through art. It was very satisfying to feel the creative power at work within oneself; but a guide stood at my studio door telling me that this was not enough. We were living in times when more was required. There was still more for me to learn.

It needed the full strength of my faith to leave my studio and set out again to find the true purpose of my life.

THE BIBLE

I felt the urge to become part of a living picture, to be united in reality with my fellow men in peace and happiness, as the colours in a picture of true art.

Thus I joined a group of people having the same ideals, in an attempt to put into common life the vision that every artist tries to express in music, colours, or words. The aim of this community was a life of love and brotherhood, sharing all work and worldly goods, making a centre of spiritual harmony and joy with work, art, study, and service to mankind. Religion was the basis, an acceptance of all religions, and there were strong influences of spiritualism and occultism.

Attracted by these ideals, I was lured into my first experience of actual contact with the spiritual forces, both good and bad, that hide behind the screen of loftiest ideals. Innocently I walked into unknown dangers; wiser and more enlightened I emerged. During that period I also gained a greater knowledge of the Bible, which was read and studied daily, together with the books of Eastern religions and philosophies.

The Bible gave me more direct light and satisfying answers than any of the other books. It seemed to me to have the truth which I was seeking. I began to read it with a new understanding.

It contains the history of the Jewish people, and in that history there was one underlying theme, one predominant note, one purpose: to give to human life on earth the understanding of God's will, God's power, and God's love.

I make no attempt here to explain the beginning of human life on earth, but go back to the time when mankind walked in the ways of darkness. "And God saw that the wickedness of man was great in the earth, and that every imagination of the thoughts of his heart was evil continually."

Then one righteous man was chosen, through whom a better way of life would be demonstrated, and all the rest were destroyed.

And God said to Noah and his sons: "Behold, I establish my covenant with you, and with your seed after you."

Again, some generations later, he said to Abraham: "I will make of thee a great nation and I will bless thee."

That was the beginning of the history of the Jews, and the education of mankind. Throughout the generations that followed God worked in this way. He chose and separated a group of people from the midst of the nations; he took one man out of this group and used him as a mouthpiece to make his laws and commandments known to mankind.

FOREFATHERS

When God made the covenant with Abraham the mission of the people of Israel began. It was not a political or an economic mission—it was a spiritual mission. Abraham and his seed were to be a great nation; not as a worldly power, but because God was their teacher. There could be no greater lesson than to be led and taught by the Creator of the universe, according to his divine law, directed toward the happiness of his creatures.

The knowledge of the blessing that was to come to the peoples of the earth was first revealed, in the school of Israel, to Abraham. After being chosen to receive this knowledge, he was tested. He passed the test of obedience when he willingly left his country, his kindred, and his father's house, and went into an unknown country. He passed the test of faith by being willing to sacrifice to God the greatest treasure and joy of his life—his son Isaac.

Isaac and Jacob were the faithful fathers of the following generations. Jacob and his seed were led into Egypt through Joseph; thus the power of the God of Israel was shown in the land of another nation. Then Moses was called to lead the people out of bondage into the land that God had promised to Abraham and his seed. On the way, in the wilderness, God gave the commandments, the laws that would separate the children of Israel from the ways of the heathen, and teach them how to live according to his will. They were to be unto him "a kingdom of priests, and a holy nation."

LAWS OF LOVE

The essence of all the commandments was: to love God and to love and respect one's neighbour; to do nothing that would harm or cause suffering, to ask nothing more than was given by God.

Diverse divine laws and ordinances dealt with every problem of human life. How much wisdom, justice, and love were shown in these laws, we can see if we take only one or two as examples:

> If thou meet thine enemy's ox or his ass going astray, thou shalt surely bring it back to him again.

If thou lend money to any of my people that is poor by thee, thou shalt not be to him as an usurer.

When thou gatherest the grapes of thy vineyard, thou shalt not glean it afterward: it shall be for the stranger, for the fatherless and for the widow.

When thou buildest a new house then thou shalt make a battlement for thy roof, that thou not bring blood upon thine house if any man fall from thence.

What love is shown in these laws! Love for the enemy, in caring even for his ox. Love for the poor by the way in which he should be lent money. Love for the stranger by letting him help himself in your vineyard. Love for your family by the care with which you build your house.

Many of the laws deal with problems of those days that no longer exist, but the spirit underlying all the laws was the same. It was also shown what judgement went with these laws, what blessing would come to those who obeyed them and what punishment to those who disobeyed.

Through this difficult school the people of Israel were compelled to go. They rebelled, they turned away, they disobeyed, but again and again they were called back. Each generation was given new leaders, teachers, prophets.

Repeatedly they were shown what was required of them. Throughout their whole history they were blessed or cursed, rewarded or punished, as they obeyed or disobeyed the will of God, followed the leaders inspired by the Spirit of God or disowned their words.

For the priests and kings the same law applied. The higher the office the greater the mission, the greater also the responsibility. The price for disobedience had always to be paid. Even Moses, the man of God, that great leader—whom the LORD knew "face to face"—could not escape payment for his one sin of taking the power of God in his own name, when he smote the rock at the waters of Meribah-Kadesh. "Because you sanctified me not in the midst of the children of Israel."

For that transgression he was not allowed to enter into the promised land. God had said to him:

> Thou shalt see the land before thee, but thou shalt not go thither into the land which I give the children of Israel.

A SPECIAL MISSION

From this I learned that the spiritual laws applying to human life were as inexorable as the natural laws that governed the universe. It was very satisfying to discover that there was the certainty of blessing in obedience to God's will. It was very frightening to see that even Moses, who was fully aware of that fact, was caught in an unguarded moment, and had to pay the penalty.

How could we who knew God only from afar ever hope to have the strength to obey his laws, when even he had failed who had known God "face to face"?

All the laws were given to bring happiness and peace to mankind, but how could we find the strength to obey those laws and have that happiness? This was not clear to me.

I continued my search. Throughout the lives of the fathers, the kings, the teachers, and prophets, there was the constant repetition of the same teaching, the same law applying, the same judgment—in individual life, and in the life of the community. The same weaknesses and failures occurred repeatedly—the willfulness and disobedience that brought one disaster after another in the course of Israel's history.

But another thing also became very apparent to me. In spite of the many weaknesses and failures, in spite of the waywardness and obstinacy, in spite of the disasters and punishments, the power of God was shown mightily at work amongst the people of Israel. He had made them his school on earth, he had provided them with prophets and teachers. He had given them a special mission. He had made his plan for them and through them. It had to be fulfilled.

It was not easy to be in this school. Much easier to be outside, to follow the gods of one's own making. Much easier not to be burdened with such responsibility, such a mission, requiring the sacrifices of all one's worldly desires, demanding constant vigilance and unfailing obedience to commandments that opposed all the ways arising from the thoughts and imaginations of the heart of man:

> For my thoughts are not your thoughts, neither are your ways my ways, saith the LORD. For as the heavens are higher than the earth, so are my ways higher than your ways, and my thoughts than your thoughts.

The hearts of many failed to be reformed, and they were cast out of the school, but those who endured the chastisement of God and returned to stand upon the rock of faith received great comfort and encouragement. To them he held out the vision of that which he would accomplish:

> And I will rejoice in Jerusalem and joy in my people. The voice of weeping shall no more be heard in her, nor the voice of crying.

> For the earth shall be full of the knowledge of the LORD, as the waters cover the sea.

Therein lay the promise that the day would come when the whole earth would live according to the will of God, and all the laws would be obeyed; there would be no longer any struggle in fulfilling them. Man would open his heart to God, and wonders would be revealed greater than anything that has yet been known on earth:

> For since the beginning of the world men have not heard, nor perceived by the ear, neither hath the eye seen, O God, beside Thee, what He hath prepared for him that waiteth for him.

FALLING SHORT

But there was also the vision of life on earth preceding that time, which is the result of mankind's rejection of a higher will, and their failure to obey the commandments. That picture is so terrible that only those can bear to look at it whose faith can stand up to the greatest tests and whose vision of the ultimate goal is very clear.

Those who turn away from the picture of the inevitable end of man's reign are blind also to the picture of life under the government of God. Their hearts are not yet able to open to him. "Do they not provoke themselves to the confusion of their own faces?"

The Jewish people were a stiff-necked, rebellious people, and strained at the reigns pulling them away from their own desires:

> For my people is foolish, they have not known me: they are sottish children and they have no understanding: they are wise to do evil, but to do good they have no knowledge.

They were ungrateful and quickly forgot the good things that God had done for them, how often he had saved them from the bondage of their sins, and from their enemies.

They built their altars to other gods, and did only lip service to the God of Israel. They were very punctilious about their burnt sacrifices and offerings, but less so about the commandments.

But God said to them:

> I spoke not unto your fathers, nor commanded them concerning burnt offerings or sacrifices: but this thing commanded I them—obey my voice and I will be your God and ye shall be my people.

> But they hearkened not, nor inclined their ear, but walked in the counsels and in the imaginations of their evil heart and went backward instead of forward.

REVELATION OF LOVE

God was full of love toward this people, like a loving father trying every method to guide a foolish child. When a child will not listen to reason, not be guided by a gentle hand, he will go headlong into the foolishness of his mistakes, and when he will still not learn from the disastrous results of his mistakes, he must be taught by ruthless severity.

All God's commandments revealed the desire for happiness for his children. His patience and mercy, his guidance and protection, showed his love:

> "Like as I have watched over them to pluck up and to break down, and throw, and to destroy, and to afflict; so will I watch over them to build and to plant," saith the LORD.

It is only when we come to love God that we can also understand his fury and his anger rightly. And this love God demands from us—that we return to him. However far away we wander, he is always there, waiting for us, if we but turn back to him. However great our sin, if we but confess it and repent accepting our punishment as the effect of the transgression of a spiritual kind, his mercy blots out our iniquity and gives us another opportunity.

DIVINE DESTINY

Having come to the end of the Old Testament in my search for the truth of life, I saw very clearly that there is a Creator, a power that we call God:

> Which giveth the sun for a light by day and the ordinances of the moon and the stars for a light by night, which divideth the sea when the waves there roar: the Lord of Hosts is His name.

All that he had created on the earth was governed by laws according to a plan that was perfect in wisdom and designed for peace, harmony, beauty, and joy.

If we, like nature, would work in harmony with those laws, all would be well. Whenever we went against those laws, many ills and troubles ensued. We had no power to change the laws of nature, we could either use them constructively or abuse them, setting in motion a destructive force.

But the human race was created not only to be an unconsciously directed creature, but a conscious collaborator of higher spiritual powers manifesting themselves upon the earth. These spiritual powers were to operate on the earth through man, made in the image of God, whose ultimate destiny was to be filled with the Spirit of God.

His plan for the working out of this destiny had already reached an important stage when he separated a group of people to be schooled for this end.

I saw the struggle of man against the higher powers of the spiritual world, for natural laws could not progress without the knowledge and command of spiritual law.

All these things seemed very clear to me. My faith was strengthened, my understanding of the mission of the Jewish people became clearer.

EXILE

It is thousands of years since those laws and commandments were given. Are we any nearer to obeying them? Is there any greater measure of peace and joy on earth today?

The people of Israel continued in disobedience and sin. They refused to learn the lessons given to them. They were punished, their temple destroyed, their land given to strangers; they were scattered amongst the nations in all the countries of the world. They worshipped other gods, they were persecuted and tortured. But they were never wholly destroyed. All through the generations, from Abraham to the present time, the power of God was at work amongst the Jewish people—and it is so today.

The Jewish people who were scattered are being gathered again, and brought back to the promised land, according to the promise of God. But where are the God-inspired teachers and leaders in Israel today? Where is the difference between life in Israel from that of any other nation?

MESSIAH

We are told through Isaiah, that a leader will arise upon whom the Spirit of God rests. "In that day the LORD shall set his hand again the second time to recover the remnant of his people. I will make you a name and a praise among all people of the earth when I turn back your captivity before your eyes, saith the LORD. I will make a new covenant with the House of Israel … I will put my law in their inward parts and write it in their hearts, and they shall all know me, from the least of them to the greatest of them. For I will forgive their iniquity and remember their sin no more."

Yet we still have to face the day of our judgment, for "Behold, the day cometh that shall burn as an oven and all the proud and all that do wickedly shall be stubble … it shall leave them neither root nor branch."

> But unto you that fear my name, shall the Sun of Righteousness arise with healing in His wings.

The Old Testament closes with the words:

> Remember ye the law of Moses my servant, which I commanded unto him on Horeb for all Israel, with the statutes and judgements.

> Behold I will send you Elijah the prophet before the coming of the great and dreadful day of the LORD, and he shall turn the hearts of the fathers to the children, and the hearts of the children to their fathers, lest I come and smite the earth with a curse.

I closed the Old Testament with the certainty of the future kingdom of God on earth; but how were we human beings to learn to obey the commandments of God? How were we to be delivered from the fetters of our transgressions? How were we to escape the consuming fire on the day of judgment?

In the whole of the history of the Jewish people in the Old Testament there was not one man who had been able to obey the commandments completely. The greatest of the prophets was only a weak human being, an imperfect instrument.

THE NEW TESTAMENT

Then I opened the New Testament in a further search for enlightenment. I had been told that all light on the Jewish way was held within the pages of the Old Testament. The New Testament was not the word of God spoken to the Jews. It was a Gentile religion.

I made many vital discoveries that contradicted this saying, and from the pages of the New Testament there was revealed to me the answers to many problems that had confused me in the Old, and many clouds were lifted. It was the continuation of the Jewish history.

It contains the story of Yeshua of Nazareth, a Jew born amongst Jews, who spoke to the Jews, who showed the Jews a way of life by which all the laws of God would be fulfilled.

He taught people the meaning of the commandments by the example of his own life. He faced the temptations of all the weaknesses of man, and conquered them in the power of God:

> For he shall know to refuse the evil and choose the good.

The motive behind all the commandments given by Moses, was love. Yeshua possessed that love and explained the law in the spirit of love, and by the example of love. He did not negate the law. He only showed the way to fulfill it. He said: "Till heaven and earth pass, one jot or one tittle shall in no way pass from the law till all be fulfilled."

Adam was the first man into whom the Spirit of God was breathed. Yeshua was the first man on whom the Spirit of God rested fully.

Moses was the first prophet and teacher guided by the Spirit of God in the school of the chosen people. Yeshua was the first prophet in whom the power of God was fully manifested on earth.

Through him the way to life with God was made clearer, and a new door was opened. He was constantly repeating that the works he did and the power he had were not his own, but those of his Father the Creator, the God of Israel. Through him the line had been crossed from the inability of man to obey God's commandments, to the positive manifestations of obedience to God's will—from death to life.

Obedience to, and fulfilment of God's commandments had shown God and man as one. Yeshua did only what the Father showed him to do. He always said he could do "nothing of himself." No ordinary human being could have done this. One had to come from the spheres of God, entering this world, not in the natural way, but in a special, divinely ordained manner—as the Son of God.

As a father loves an obedient son and shows him all he knows, so God gave all his powers to Yeshua. He healed the sick, gave sight to the blind, raised the dead, calmed the storm, and did many things that could not be done in human power. Only one sent by God could perform such miracles.

This was the greatest step forward toward the goal and fulfilment of the Jewish mission.

A NEW LIGHT

How thrilled I was as this realisation dawned on me! The New Testament showed me indeed the continuation, the fulfilment of all that was in the Old Testament—a vital part of the history of the Jews.

It was as though one veil after another was lifted from my eyes; one door after another was opened until I walked on and on into eternity, the torchbearer of eternal life guiding me step by step.

Just as in the days of Noah, and later throughout the generations of teachers and prophets—only a few could listen and follow the one inspired by God; so also at the time of Yeshua, only a few chosen Jews could follow in faith this new light that was given to them. This light was the most powerful that had yet come to the earth. The ruling Jews therefore feared its power to penetrate the dark places in which they hid their self-indulgence behind the mask of law and justice; for the priests and leaders of those days had hardened themselves with the laws written in gilded letters, but the spirit was imprisoned behind the bars of self-love and pride.

It was "the rod of his mouth" that smote them: "the breath of his lips" that slew them. They had no power against him and so they sought to remove him by death.

Little did they know what powers in heaven and on earth would be moved by the shedding of that blood! Blind to the significance of his life, they were unable to understand the miracle of his death.

There was found no guile and no sin in this man Yeshua, who was sentenced to death on the cross by the wish of his own people. He went to his death, bearing in the purity of his blood the sins of his people and the sins of mankind.

He was made in the form of man, filled with the Spirit of God; he was the Son of God and the son of man, and through the power that was given to him by the Father, he led the way for us all to become sons and daughters of God.

He offered his life, a life without blemish, as a sacrifice for the sins of mankind, and for the deliverance of his people on the way to fulfilling their mission. He was their brother, their leader, their saviour.

AN OPEN DOOR

With the death and resurrection of Yeshua, a new way was shown, and it was possible for all to walk in it. The door is open; we only need to follow the one who opened it, and has stood there ever since, to lead us through.

In Isaiah we are told: "And an highway shall be there, and a way, and it shall be called the way of holiness; the unclean shall not pass over it; but it shall be there for those: the wayfaring men, though fools, shall not err therein."

There is the way, which Yeshua showed us—the way of love. And it will lead us to the highway of God, where nothing unclean can live. All who seek that way, ready to sacrifice all things, even unto death—though they be called fools for doing so—will never be mistaken, but will return to their God and "come to Zion with songs and everlasting joy upon their heads"—and in their hearts.

WHERE IS THE KINGDOM?

It was difficult for me to understand why life had not changed after two thousand years; and I hear you saying, dear friend, "If sin and death have been conquered by Yeshua, why is the earth still so steeped in wickedness? Where is there any sign of the fulfilment of the Jewish mission and the kingdom of God on earth?"

Yeshua opened the door and made the way possible, and he called: "Follow me." But how many have followed him? The Jews rejected and crucified him.

Only a very small number followed him and learned from him. To these few he revealed the secret of his death and the reality of his resurrection; to them his spirit was given, also the power to work miracles, to heal and to save; to receive the grace of eternal life and to enter into the kingdom of God. They were shown in what manner it will be established on earth.

Those few Jews who followed Yeshua were the first bricks laid upon the foundation stone, in the building of the kingdom. They recognised in Yeshua, the promised Messiah, the deliverer and King of Israel.

ISRAEL AND THE KINGDOM

The message of Yeshua was also brought to the Gentiles. For two thousand years the gospel of the New Testament has been known in the world, and preached under the name of Christianity. But just as with the people of Israel, so also among the nations, only a few really believed and obeyed Messiah. The rest used the cloak of Christianity for selfish ends, and even to cover the darkest deeds. The way of the cross was still rejected by the peoples of the earth.

Yet it is Israel that is to be the holy nation, in whom the other nations of the world are to see the beacon of God—showing the way to all mankind.

If we want to know how near we are to the day of God's kingdom on earth, we must see what God is doing with the Jewish people. The prophets of old tell us of the terrible things that will happen during the working out of the plan, until finally a new covenant will be established, and the laws of God written, not only in printed letters, but in the heart of every man, woman, and child.

About the coming of this time we are given further revelation in the New Testament.

"For then shall be great tribulation, such as was not since the beginning of the world to this time, no, nor ever shall be."

Then there is the promise of the return of the Messiah, who will come in great power and glory—the setting up of the kingdom on earth. We are told of many signs that will signal the approaching day of the Lord. But, "the day and hour knoweth no man, not even the angels in heaven, but my father only," said Yeshua.

We are told to watch and be prepared.

CHAPTER TWO

THE LIGHT OF THE MESSIAH

I f we wish to trace the development and progress of the Messianic Jewish community, we must follow the Sabbath light, which is kindled in honour of the Messiah, the Lord of the Sabbath. When the appointed time in God's plan had come for the forming of the Messianic Jewish community, his Spirit worked in the hearts and minds of those he had chosen, while they were as yet unknown to one another. Each one was being prepared for his task. The stones were being matched and chiselled to fit together for the foundation of the Messianic synagogue in Israel. The light of the Messiah was to burn in the hearts of those who, waiting for his return, were ready to receive him as their King and Saviour.

Many great trials and tests in the personal lives of the individuals chosen led them along different paths, converging, however, toward the central point—the vision of the crucified and risen Yeshua, the Messiah of Israel, and of his promised return. With that revelation came the acceptance of his leadership and the deep desire to serve him.

FIRST STEPS

The call first came to Abram Poljak in 1935 when he had the vision of the Messianic synagogue and of the mission to prepare the way for the return of Yeshua and the setting up of the kingdom of God on earth. For years he walked alone along that path, facing all manner of opposition and criticism—the path of a pioneer.

Meanwhile, others, also traveling the lonely road, answered a call that was to bring them together to form a community—to kindle the Sabbath light of the Messiah, the preparation for the Messianic congregation in Israel.

In 1937, the first four members met in London, each one from a different country, each as diverse in temperament as were the backgrounds and experiences through which they had passed in preparation for this mission.

SEPARATION AND REUNION

With this beginning of a movement destined to carry the torch of the Messiah in Israel, began the battle in which the dark powers of the world sought firstly to prevent its light being kindled, or failing that, to make continued attempts to extinguish it. For the recognition and acceptance of the Messiah in Israel marks the nearness of his return and the end of this age of wars and evil. The trials within the Community were accompanied by the battles outside. When war was declared in 1939, it had serious effect upon the young community.

Three of its members were interned as enemy aliens in Britain. Abram Poljak spent three years behind a barbed wire fence in a Canadian camp, while the others were held in different locations. Thus the community was broken up, its members separated, deprived of mutual support and fellowship; but a work started by God cannot be thwarted. He had chosen his instruments for his purposes, and they were strengthened in the fire of adversity in order to further his plan.

In 1944, the period of separation came to an end. The four members were reunited in London and went forward again together toward the next step in the development of the work. They became entirely dependent upon their Leader, their Messiah. The centre of the group's faith, the significance of its purpose, the vision of its future, was to be symbolised in its form of worship. The light of the Messiah, which had been rejected by the synagogue and failed in the churches, was to be kindled anew in a synagogue built by the Messiah himself, where *he* was the high priest, and where *his* congregation would worship.

THE SYNAGOGUE OF THE MESSIAH

At this point another chosen servant of God was led into the community. Nathan Whycer, a rabbi, trained in the Orthodox Jewish tradition, had received the revelation of the Messiah, and was guided to compose the liturgy. At the first Sabbath service of the Messianic Jewish community he officiated, and continued to do so during the following nine months until his early death. He had accomplished his mission, being faithful unto death.

On the sixth day of the week, as the sun disappears, Jewish people all over the world celebrate the arrival of the Sabbath. In every Jewish home two candles are lit with the words: "Blessed are you, O LORD our God, King of the universe, who has sanctified us with his commandments and has commanded us to observe the Sabbath."

On June 16, 1944, the eve of the Sabbath, a small Jewish community and some of their Gentile friends gathered together in a humble room on the top floor of a tenement house in the East End of London, to hold the traditional Jewish service of the inauguration of the Sabbath; but for the first time the Sabbath light was "kindled in honour of Yeshua the Messiah, the Lord of the Sabbath"—a light never to be extinguished. This first Sabbath service in the community marked an important step in the development of its work.

THE SPIRITUAL HOME

It was to one of these Friday evening services that I was guided, and the sincere spirit of truth and love that I found in that small gathering showed me that my search for a spiritual home was ended. I had found brethren with whom I was to work from then on in a common spiritual calling.

The synagogue of the Messiah, which was still in its beginnings, did not have a permanent location. The building would be erected in the hearts of the men and women equally without a fixed residence, moving from place to place according to the calling they received. This is why the Sabbath light also moved from place to place. In whichever temporary location that this small group of believers possessed, they held services every Friday evening. Many different friends gathered together around this light, Jews and Gentiles. Some came only once, others remained united with us for some time and then left us. Many were called but only a few were chosen to keep the light burning, and to guard it.

JERUSALEM

In 1946, the time had come for the Sabbath light of the Messiah to be kindled in the Holy Land. The two years in London had been a preparation for this important step.

I was chosen for this particular mission. Being the one with the least experience on the spiritual battlefield, I went innocently into the unknown dangers of Jerusalem. But God chooses his instruments with wisdom. Had I had known something of the dangers and the opposition I was to encounter, my courage might have failed me. I would have been tempted to fight with my own wisdom. In this way I would have fallen, with eyes closed, and without relying completely on God, into numerous traps. As for my wisdom and capability, they did not provide me any support, so much so that Yeshua himself took my hand and led me through the enemy's camps.

For four months I searched in all Christian and Messianic Jewish circles of Palestine for those who shared our vision, the vision of Yeshua in the synagogue. I was always received warmly and enthusiastically at first, but when I spoke of our Sabbath service and my hope of kindling the Sabbath light of the Messiah in the Holy Land, I was met with the strongest opposition on all sides.

Certain groups considered it their duty to protect me against this "satanic faith." Others attempted to direct my "misguided" steps toward the "only truth," which could be found only in their church or particular sect [of Christianity]. Each made a concerted effort to "save my soul," putting me on guard against the Sabbath lighting, saying that the Sabbath service—a Jewish custom and not a Christian one—would pull me down into the depths of hell. They seemed to think that any connection with the Jewish people, the law or the synagogue, would lead me to destruction. It was as though it had been forgotten that Yeshua was a Jew, that he had shown that the Law must be fulfilled, that he had preached in the synagogue, and that he would return to his Jewish people.

The powers of darkness are very strong in Jerusalem, and had the hand of Yeshua not held me firmly, I would certainly have broken down or lost my mental balance in the fight around the kindling of the light of the Messiah.

An influential group of Christians, who were self-proclaimed guardians of the Holy City, threatened to chase me out of the country, asserting that neither I, nor any other member of our community, would ever again be permitted to enter Jerusalem.

At that time, perhaps more than at any other, I realised my utter helplessness and weakness in the face of the enemy; but I was also conscious of the wonders and the power of Messiah. I was carried through all the attacks and finally led to the Mount of Olives, from whence Yeshua ascended to heaven, and where, we believe, he will return.

There, on June 22, 1946, in a small room in an Arab house, I kindled the Sabbath light of the Messiah for the first time in Jerusalem. This date marks the foundation of the Synagogue of the Messiah in the Holy City. The second important step on the way of our mission had been taken, just two years after the first Sabbath service had been held in London.

Ten people witnessed the first kindling of the light on the Mount of Olives. A small community was formed. Satan attempted by all means to extinguish that light. Only three of the ten people remained with us throughout all the storms. The faith was tested, weaknesses were laid bare, and Satan used all means to extinguish that light. However, although the Community was badly shaken and nearly broken up, the light continued to burn; no wind could extinguish it.

WAR

In 1947, at the commencement of the siege of Jerusalem, it seemed as though the storms might prove too strong for us. Not only did we have to face the enemy around us, but his power worked also within our ranks. Certain members of the Community, who were invited to help lead services, suggested that they remove themselves until the dangers of war had passed. There were fears and doubts, bullets, shells, and all the influences of war. However, the light was kindled every Sabbath eve, and the peace of Sabbath and the power of the light of the Messiah brought comfort and strengthening to the Community and all its friends. The light of Messiah shone brightly in Israel—in Jerusalem, even during its darkest days.

THE NEW RESIDENCE

In the first days of 1949, after having wandered from place to place, the Community received a new home: a place situated on the Mount of Olives, which became the dedicated sanctuary of the community. The Sabbath light could be illuminated there in peace, under the protection of the Messiah of Israel.

There it has burned undisturbed until the present, and continues to attract, to test, to sift the weak in faith, and to strengthen those who are chosen for this mission.

If we follow that Sabbath light, we see the development of the Community. Looking back to its beginning in 1937, or even further back to the vision of Abram Poljak, we can see how many were called into it and how few chose to remain.

Today [1951] those who have remained faithful from the beginning carry on the work of the Messianic Jewish Community.

As it is with our Jewish members, so it is also with our Gentile brethren. Many joined us with enthusiasm and left us with doubts and fears. The Sabbath services showed who truly belonged to this work. Those who support us and have remained faithful suffer criticism and often separation; for anyone who shares our calling also shares the difficulties and attacks which beset us on our path.

LAST YEAR

Looking over the past year reveals nothing particularly sensational in our work or in our development. We are frequently asked: "How are you coming along? Has your work in Israel been successful?" Our response is this: "We are doing nothing else but maintaining the ignited flame. We are not successful in the world's eyes. Few people come to us, and just as few people leave us."

What can we say about that which has transpired in our community in Jerusalem and here in London? What can we do? Or better, what is God doing through us? This past year in London was marked by an increase in numbers and a deepening of faith. There were trials, and none of us were spared from Satan's influences; however, the enemy does not have weapons that are strong enough to pierce the breastplate of repentance and faith. The Sabbath light continues to shine in our midst and we enjoy an even greater spiritual union, a testament to the unity of Jews and Gentiles in the Messiah. We can see the *whole* "family"—the children of God—where every barrier is torn down, and in this small family of Jews and Gentiles we see the sign of the fulfillment of the future promise: true brotherly love amongst all of humanity in the kingdom of God.

THE TASK

The task of keeping the light burning in Jerusalem in the midst of Israel is a great and difficult one; demanding unwavering faith and complete dependence on God. Those to whom that task has been allotted are the ones with whom the Community was first formed in London. Each one has been tested and tried since the beginning of this work. They followed the call and were guided step by step out of different countries, to the meeting place in London, and from London one by one to Jerusalem, the centre of Israel. As the powers of darkness make their last frantic effort for dominion on this earth, still greater attempts will be made to extinguish the light of the Messiah and to destroy the bearers of that light.

What has God been doing with us? He has been testing us, strengthening us, welding us together more firmly. Quietly our Leader has trained us, moulding us into instruments to prepare for the coming of his kingdom. We do not know what the next call will be, nor what task will be given us. But we can see the importance of the kindling of the Sabbath light, which has guided us from a tenement house in the East End of London to the Mount of Olives. Only once, the first time, was the light kindled on that sacred hill. Now we are not able to go there, as it is within Arab-held territory; but one day we, or our successors, will be there again, not to kindle his light but to welcome the Messiah himself, the Light of the World, whose presence will illumine the whole earth and penetrate every heart.

ON THE WAY

Until now we have travelled only part of the way, and there will be still greater trials awaiting us. We know that God's work will go on. We have learned also that whoever is not prepared to surrender his whole life to God in this calling will be put aside. Perhaps our numbers will diminish instead of grow, and even though we have been able to arrive at this point on the journey it is not certain that we will not fall when new obstacles block our way. We must ever be watchful and ready.

In Israel a few Jews have gathered together to carry the torch of the Messiah. In other countries some Gentiles have been chosen to uphold the light in the midst of the nations. Let us march together in unity, supporting and strengthening one another in love and prayer.

The forces of the world will try to separate us from the light of Messiah. The last step of the expedition will be more difficult than the first, but those who persevere until the end will meet him (the Messiah). Those who have conceded to be transformed into one of his instruments will be used by him in the establishment of his kingdom. Allow us to yet recall the words that we recite when lighting the Sabbath flame: "Arise, shine, for your light has come and the glory of the LORD has shone upon you," and "Let your light shine before men so that they will see your good works and give praise to your Father who is in heaven."

VICTORY

Although our Community is small at present, let us not be discouraged; the time has not yet come for great numbers to be added to our ranks. The first community formed by Yeshua was also a small one; but it was filled with his power, and through that small group of faithful disciples the gospel was given to the world.

We are now at the turn of the age; all signs point to the nearness of the return of the Messiah. Once again he has gathered together a small community in preparation for the day of his coming. Until that day we cannot expect great numbers of believers in Israel. Only when he returns *the whole nation* will see "him whom they pierced and will mourn for him." In that day, too, "many nations will turn to God." That will be our day of victory; then our Community will no longer be a small one; it will be great in numbers and in power.

Let us keep this vision clear and bright, following the light that has been given to us, looking neither to the right nor to the left, but remaining steadfast to the end—until the goal is reached.

CHAPTER THREE

THE MISSION OF THE MESSIANIC JEWISH COMMUNITY

The name "Messianic Jewish Community" usually raises a number of queries in the minds of those who hear it for the first time: What is the Messianic Jewish Community?[15] Why should there be a Messianic Jewish Community? What is the purpose and mission of the Messianic Jewish Community?

We would reply to these questions by saying:

1. We are a community of Jews who believe Yeshua of Nazareth to be the Messiah of Israel, the Saviour of the world; we remain united with our Jewish people, not becoming members of any Gentile church.

2. We believe that we are called into being to be a group witness for our faith in Israel and to be a spiritual centre and home for all Jews who seek the Messiah.

3. Our mission is to rekindle the light of the Messiah in the synagogue and to proclaim the message of the kingdom to the Jews and to all nations. We believe that the return of the Messiah is very near, and our message is a call to all Christians to unite

---

15 Jewish Christian Community. See introduction.

under the banner of the Messiah in Israel, and prepare the way to his kingdom.

MESSIANIC JEWS

We stand in a peculiar position today being rejected by both Jew and Gentile. The Jews cannot accept a Messianic Jew. They say that if a Jew becomes a Christian he is a traitor to his people and is no longer a member of the Jewish nation. The Gentiles say that when a Jew becomes a believer he should become a member of one of the existing Gentile churches and be absorbed by the church and nation in which he finds himself.

Thus both sides urge the Messianic Jew to renounce his ties with the nation of Israel. The church does not require a Frenchman or a Spaniard or an Indian to sever his connection with his people when he becomes a Christian, nor does a Jew who becomes a theosophist or a spiritualist or a communist cease to be a Jew; Yeshua—the crucified and risen Messiah—is the stumbling block (1 Corinthians 1: 23).

It is often said by Gentile Christians: Why should there be a separate Messianic Jewish Community to add to the numerous Christian communities that already exist?

THE ORIGINAL CHRISTIANS

It seems to be forgotten that the first Christian community was an entirely Jewish one, formed by Yeshua himself, who was a Jew and never severed his connection with his people or negated the law of Judaism, but came to Israel as their promised Messiah, to fulfil the Law completely.

The first church was a Jewish church, a synagogue in which Yeshua preached and in which later his disciples preached the gospel of Messiah. The gospel was then passed on to the Gentiles, not because Israel and the synagogue were to be rejected in God's plan; but they were to be set aside only for a time, for a period during which grace was given to the Gentiles and the mission of preaching the gospel of salvation passed on to the Gentile church.

RETURN OF THE MESSIANIC JEWISH COMMUNITY

From that time until now there has been no Jewish church, no synagogue in which the gospel, the message of the kingdom, has been preached. There have been individual Jews throughout the centuries who received the revelation of Messiah as the Saviour of the world, but as there was no spiritual home for them amongst their people, they either joined the Gentile church or remained lonely and unacknowledged by both Jew and Gentile.

For two thousand years this has been the accustomed way of Christianity in the world, and has come to be accepted generally as the only way. It is like many other things shaped by the spirit for a particular function, taking a visible form that is retained by habit long after the spirit has left it and its function has been fulfilled.

So it is with the Gentile church today. Its form remains but its function is coming to an end, the power of the spirit is leaving it. Because the mission of the Gentile church has been a form so familiar as to become almost a habit, not requiring any new thought or action, the appearance of a Jewish Christian Movement causes a disturbance on these smooth unruffled waters. Why the need to be disturbed?

The fact that a Messianic Jewish Community appears again in our time, continuing in the way of the first Messianic Jewish Community is indeed something that demands attention. Is it not the most significant sign that the "fullness of the Gentiles be come in" and that the "blindness in part" that happened to Israel is beginning to be removed?

Those who do not wish to be disturbed on their accustomed path reject it, fight against it, and return to the comfort of their established niche in the scheme of things handed down to them. Others listen with reservation, not wishing to enter into any battle, but preferring to remain in familiar surroundings. Then there are those who read their Bibles with eyes opened by faith, and long before the appearance of the Messianic Jewish Community, waited for this sign from God that his grace was returning to his people Israel, that he was preparing them for the return of the Messiah into their midst, to establish his kingdom on earth. These, chosen by God to rejoice with his people, were the ones who prayed for us while we were still traversing the difficult path that led us to our Messiah; who greeted us with joy, with love and understanding when we appeared; who by their prayers and faith have helped us to receive the power to remain firm in our faith, united in love and prepared to follow our Messiah to the end—to the day of his return.

A TWO-FOLD MISSION

Our mission is two-fold: to the Jews and to the Gentiles. Our Community is established in Jerusalem, where the synagogue of Messiah appears once more in Israel, continuing in direct succession to the first Jewish church. That is the centre of our work, where the light of the Messiah is kindled. It is a spiritual home for the lonely ones who have confessed their faith in Yeshua and are misunderstood by Jew and Gentile alike. It is also a home where help and support are given in time of need, both spiritual and material, and it is a centre of prayer, where channels are opened up for the healing and blessing of Israel and the nations.

In this country and others, it is our mission to proclaim the message of the kingdom, the urgency of the times in which we live, when all signs point to the nearness of the return of Messiah. It is a call to all Christians to abandon those things that cause division, and dwell only upon the things that unite—to be made one in the redemptive blood of Messiah. It is also a call to prayer.

The message of the Messianic Jewish Community in these days disturbs and separates. It disturbs those who dislike being shaken out of their spiritual torpor and numbness; it separates those who do not wish to take the Word of God seriously from those who accept the prophecies as God's promises to Israel, and have faith in their complete fulfilment in God's appointed time.

In this way it divides, but its mission is to unite all who have been given the vision of the approaching kingdom of God on earth. The Messianic Jewish Community is one with all Christians everywhere who share this vision, no matter to what church, religious group, or nation they belong. We have the promise that when Messiah returns all Israel will see him as their Messiah and King, and through Israel all the families of the earth will be blessed. The Messianic Jewish Community is the beginning of Israel's salvation.

Today we are only a few, forming a bridge leading from the time of the Gentiles to the kingdom of Israel. John the Baptist preached the first coming of the Lord in Israel; we preach the second coming, and with his words we call: "Repent ye, for the kingdom of God is at hand." The Messianic Jewish Community is a community of Jews, separated for its particular mission, but the Jewish Christian Brotherhood of the kingdom founded in Basle in 1952 is the development of the movement embracing Christians from every denomination and every race, a movement that begins in the last days of this age and leads to the beginning of the coming—the Millennial Kingdom.

CHAPTER FOUR

OUR PROTECTION

Thank are many storms ahead of us. As we said before: "The last part of the way will be more difficult than the first." The battlefield is prepared: the opposing sides are being called out and separated. In Israel the soldiers of God have taken the first step into the open, where they will meet the enemy face to face.

Our most powerful protection in this battle is prayer. This also is part of our responsibility—to pray for one another and for ourselves, for guidance in all we do. Prayer is our link with God, our contact with heavenly powers. Some of us are called to go out into the world to speak, some to write, some to minister to the material needs of the community while others bear the small daily burdens. Whatever our task may be, one thing is necessary for all of us—to be in constant communion with God, to "pray without ceasing." The prayers of a loving heart offered up in the spirit of the Messiah are heard and answered by God. They build a wall of protection around us in all dangers and storms.

For this purpose God calls together his soldiers in all countries, to form a united front against the enemy in the days of his last battle, and to be channels of blessing for the world. It is a call to those who are prepared to give their lives in service to God, to unite and rally around the banner of Messiah in Israel—to prepare the way for his kingdom.

With our feet set firmly on the path marked by the spiritual signposts, bearing our responsibility faithfully, we will march on toward our goal, rejoicing in the midst of all trials, as we prepare to welcome the One who will come to meet us, the Holy One of Israel. "Yet a little while, and He that shall come will come, and will not tarry" (Hebrews 10:37).

PART II

THE SIEGE
OF JERUSALEM

CHAPTER FIVE

TOWARD EVENING

1946–1947

At the end of 1945 I received a letter from Jerusalem from my sister who was in Palestine on a visit from South Africa. She asked me to meet her there as we had not seen one another for some years. I was living at the time at Heston Farm, a peaceful oasis of green cultivated land not far from London.

TWO WORLDS

My sister's suggestion fired the desire within me to see Palestine, and on the 18th of March 1946, I said farewell to my family and friends, and sailed from Southampton on my first visit to the land of my people. It was a dull rainy day, and as the ship left the harbour the coastline of England was soon lost behind the misty grey mantle that enveloped land, sea, and sky.

Seven days later I landed at Port Said, where the warmth and brilliance of the sunlight were dazzling. I stepped into a world of light, colour, warmth, noise, and confusion. From there I went to Kantara, where I crossed the Suez Canal. It was a warm fragrant night, and the stars, leaving no place in the sky unoccupied, seemed to be suspended tantalisingly above my head, as though an outstretched hand could touch them. As I sat waiting in the ferry I realised that only the narrow strip of water divided me from

Palestine; and when a little later I stepped off the ferry—I stood on the soil of the Holy Land.

At dawn the next morning the passing scenes through the train window were fascinating. Prickly pear hedges framed fields where camels pulled the plough, followed by long-robed Arabs with flowing head-dress. Dark palms were silhouetted against a pearly, rose-tinted sky; tall, graceful white trunks of eucalyptus trees showed their cascades of long, dark leaves.

A narrow pathway wound its way through the silvery olive trees where a long-robed, dark-skinned man was carried leisurely along on the back of a small donkey. As the sun rose higher in the heavens I saw large groves of orange trees weighed down by the golden fruit, ripe for picking. There were banana trees, fig trees, mimosa trees yellow with blossom; and beyond narrow strips of green country—the golden sands of the desert, an undulating line against the blue cloudless sky. A camel caravan, a woman filling her pitcher at a well, and then—prefabricated metal huts, armoured cars, a military camp!

From Lydda we passed through the mountains, mostly bare and barren with occasional Arab villages nestling on the hillside, looking as though they were cut out of the mountain itself. Small areas of land were terraced and cultivated, making picturesque lines and patterns of green around the hills.

THE HOLY CITY

At midday, in blazing heat and dazzling sunshine, I arrive in Jerusalem—the Holy City. My sister was waiting at the station to meet me and I was welcomed by her friends. That same afternoon I was taken for a drive to Mount Scopus, and from that height I looked down upon Jerusalem.

The Old City walls encircled a small area from which rising towers, minarets, domes, and spires were the visible signs of the invisible forces concentrated there. Outside the Old City the new one had grown, built of the same rough stone—a warm, rose-tinted yellow. New towers, domes, and minarets outside the walls united the character of the old with the new.

I stayed at the King David Hotel and the first few days were filled with visits to all the places of interest that had emerged from the new creative life in the city—the Hadassah Hospital, the University, the municipal buildings, the children's home, the private houses. I saw also the many improvements and developments in the general amenities of life.

But besides all this outward expression and visible form resulting from the creative activity that had returned to the land, I was most strongly impressed by the overwhelming spiritual forces at work in the unseen spheres.

Jerusalem, the centre, the focal point of all the spiritual streams, seemed to have above its head a crystal globe divided into many fragments; each fragment suspended above one of the diverse churches, synagogues, and mosques, imbuing them with a power that flowed out into the world and returned again to its starting point—Jerusalem.

For two months I travelled through the country visiting towns, villages, settlements, and farms. Everywhere a new life was struggling to break through the manifold obstacles and hindrances—the climate, the neglected land, the hostile Arabs, and the more subtle difficulties hidden behind the Mandatory Power. There was freedom of spirit; but freedom of action was hampered.

During the three months that I was in Palestine those hidden, subtle, hostile forces became more and more exposed. There was an ever-increasing number of clashes between individual members of the Mandatory Power and individual members of the Jewish Community.

The spiritual streams flowing into the world returned to their source more and more polluted.

UNDER ESCORT

I had difficulty in getting passage back to England. I had to wait for an opportunity. During the last week I stayed with my friend R. and her family in Jerusalem. There was a tense atmosphere of hostility in the city. Barbed wire protected the buildings occupied by the Mandatory Power. Armed British soldiers, armoured cars, and other warlike precautionary measures were apparent on all sides.

On the 29th of June 1946, at an hour between midnight and dawn, I was awakened by loud voices and the sound of motor cars and much activity in the streets. I was living in Rehavia, very near to the Jewish Agency Building.

Voices from loudspeakers making important announcements travelled through all the streets. Most of the noise and activity came from the direction of the Jewish Agency Building. After a period of restrained curiosity I went downstairs and found R's husband sitting beside his radio.

"The Jewish Agency Building has been occupied by the British, and the leaders have been arrested," he said, in answer to my look of enquiry. "There is a strict curfew throughout the city. It is forbidden to go outside the door of one's home."

As I sat at breakfast with the family that morning, there was an atmosphere of depression and anxiety. During the many years they had lived in Jerusalem they had experienced so many disturbances. Their lives had been in danger so many times. "What next?" was the unexpressed thought in each mind. "When should I be able to return to my home in London?" was one of the passing thoughts in my mind.

Before the thought had left me, the telephone rang. "British Airways!" I took the receiver from R. A voice at the other end said, "If you are prepared to leave in an hour's time, we can fix you up on a mail plane from Australia. One of the passengers is ill and must leave the plane when it arrives at Lydda. If you do not take this opportunity we can't give you much hope of any other way of getting back to England."

Half an hour later a jeep arrived at the door with a military escort. I said farewell to my dear friends. It was the Sabbath morning. As I entered the jeep there was a commotion in the street. A young man was seized by several British soldiers. There was an argument; an armoured car drove up. The young man had defied the curfew in an attempt to reach the synagogue—it was the Sabbath morning. He was taken away in an armoured car. The streets of Jerusalem were like a prepared battlefield with guns, soldiers, armoured cars, barbed wire, and barricades. All other life was behind closed doors.

The military escort accompanied the jeep to Lydda. After a few hours' wait at the airport, the plane arrived. The sick passenger was removed and I took his place. The four other passengers were men on an important government mission. The plane was a converted Lancaster bomber with good sleeping accommodations.

At seven o'clock, when the sun had already sunk below the horizon, I was lifted from the soil of the Holy Land. A few minutes later I saw the coastline beneath the grey mist that hovered over the earth; and above that the warm parting glow that the sun had left in the sky.

Then—the sea below, the heavens above—Palestine was already miles away; but within me had awakened a love that pledged itself eternally—for better or for worse!

ENGLAND AGAIN

At dawn on June 30th the plane landed at Heathrow, and I stepped out onto English soil again. Half an hour later I arrived at Heston Farm. Being unable to telegraph because of my sudden departure, I was not expected. Everyone was still asleep.

I was glad to have a little time alone in order to adjust myself to the drastic change. Only ten hours ago I had been in Palestine, in Jerusalem, the battlefield of unseen spiritual powers!

Now I was in England! I walked 'round the garden of Cherry Tree Cottage. The rose bushes were covered with fragrant blooms, and many different flowers displayed their beauty in neat flowerbeds and in corners of unrestrained freedom. I walked through the orchards under trees heavy with blossom, and through the farmland, where various shades of green made lines upon the warm, tinted earth. I looked in at the glasshouses, where heavy trusses of ripening fruit hung from tomato plants. The tall old elm trees looked down from their height to the small tender lettuce plants below.

I returned to the cottage. Someone was awake. Very soon there were cries of surprise and joy at the unexpected reunion. I sat at the breakfast table with my family. I remembered my breakfast the day before.

It took several months to adjust myself to the change from Palestine to England. It was like coming from a mountain peak to a deep valley. The light, colour, air—everything seemed many tones lower. In Palestine there was life—struggle, battle, creation. One could feel the strength of the heartbeats. In England there was silence, a twilight, with muffled murmurings, a spiritual void—the pulse was weak.

The months passed by, and with the months the longing to return to Palestine was kept in check by the knowledge that at the appointed time, when my duties were fulfilled, I should return. Until God opened the way patience was necessary.

During those months I felt the growth of anti-Semitism in England. Every crime committed by the Jewish terrorists in Palestine was an opportunity for accusation against the whole Jewish people. The daily newspapers fed the germ that had poisoned the bodies of many nations for many generations, a poison calculated to destroy the Jews, but which ultimately destroyed the body into which it was injected.

Completely distorted pictures were given of events that I had experienced in Palestine, and when, after many requests, I arranged to speak at a meeting at Heston Farm about the life and achievements of the Jews in their own land—many who had asked me to speak stayed away. That day part of the King David Hotel had been blown up.

The newspapers injected another dose of poison against the whole Jewish people. The Jews in Palestine as well as in other parts of the world deplored the acts of violence committed by a small group within their ranks and suffered much on that account.

But the poison worked. There were attempts to burn synagogues in many parts of England. Jewish shops were raided and windows smashed. Friendships cooled, and people who had never before been conscious of Jews being any different from themselves began to ask questions. The poison of anti-Semitism was working fast in England.

PARTITION

Meanwhile the Palestine problem was a disturbing factor in world politics, and in November 1947, the United Nations Assembly decided to solve the problem by the partition plan—one part of Palestine to go to the Jews, the other to the Arabs. The decision was welcomed by the Jews and rejected by the Arabs, thus increasing the unrest that already existed in the country.

At a meeting in London where Jews gathered together to celebrate the occasion I spoke to a man who had flown from Jerusalem that day.

"There is great rejoicing amongst the Jews in all parts of Palestine," he said. "There was dancing and singing in the streets throughout the night when the news of the UN decision was received. The Jews feel that, however unsatisfactory the partition may be, they will have at least a small area of the Holy Land where they will be free from the bondage of foreign rule, free to make a home, to have a place in the world where their full rights are recognised—to have a State, a Jewish State!"

"Do they not realise the dangers?" I asked.

"They are fully aware of the difficulties that lie ahead," he replied, "of the price that will still have to be paid in spite of the right given to them by the UN decision. They are surrounded by hostile Arabs, the Mandatory Power in Palestine is not yet ended, but the Jews are tightening their belts and preparing to defend themselves and their embryo State."

CHAPTER SIX

THE DAY IS FAR SPENT

FEBRUARY–MARCH 1948

At the end of 1947, I was ready to leave England again. The situation in Palestine was very critical. All British women and children were being sent back to England. The Jews and the British had been separated and confined in different zones. The dark storm clouds were gathering, heavy-laden with the threat of war.

RETURN

The time had come for me to return to Palestine. Those nearest to me begged me to reconsider my decision and to wait until the situation in Palestine was clearer. There were many visitors to Heston Farm, and when the whisper went 'round of my intention to go to Palestine I was continually bombarded with advice to change my plan. Relatives, friends, farm workers, strangers—all were anxious. Personal visits, phone calls, letters from abroad, all contained the same "good advice"—in my interest, and out of genuine concern.

"It is madness to go at this juncture," I was told, "you will never get a visa. Why not wait until April, when the Mandatory Power ends?"

Others said, "It will be a terrible war. There will be a mass slaughter by the Arabs."

Many similar reasons were put before me in an attempt to prevent me from going so foolishly into the possibility of useless suffering and perhaps—death. But I was bound to Palestine—for better or for worse.

Very soon, to the astonishment of everyone, I received my visa and made application for a seat in a plane. At Cook's booking office the man to whom I made my request looked at me very curiously and asked, "Is it really necessary for you to go to Palestine now?"

"Yes," I replied.

"Do you fully realise the position out there?"

"Yes."

"Do you know that now there is also an outbreak of cholera?"

"Yes."

He looked at me even more curiously than before.

"Well, we can possibly book you a seat to Lydda via Geneva, but from the moment you step out of the plane at Lydda we are no longer responsible for you. We cannot guarantee transport from there, and there is no accommodation at the airport now. All rooms are occupied by British officials. You may also be kept in quarantine for many days. There have been serious clashes with the Arabs in and around Lydda recently. Lives have been lost."

"I am very grateful for your friendly concern," I replied, "and I appreciate all your warnings. When can I have air passage?"

He gave up the appeal to reason, smiled, murmured something about women being strange creatures, looked through his papers and offered me a seat in a plane the following week.

On February 10, 1948, I was again at Heathrow airport—the beginning of my journey back to Jerusalem! I spent that night in Geneva, enjoying the beauty, the atmosphere of prosperity, and the real whipped cream in my coffee—an extravagance not known in London for many years.

The following morning I entered the large Swiss airplane that took me to Palestine. The day was clear and sunny, and as it came to its end we passed through a mysterious world above the clouds, a world of fantastic colours and ethereal forms, constantly changing.

Descending from that wondrous cloud sphere I could discern the distant coastline. The daylight faded, the lights of Lydda airport guided the landing. A few minutes later I stepped out of the plane. I stood again on the soil of the Holy Land.

THE ARMOURED CAR

It was dark and muddy. There had been much rain. Together with the other passengers I entered the small office and passed through all the official checking of passports, money, and customs. An open door revealed a first-aid room, which showed signs of much use. All formalities being concluded I asked if there was a conveyance to Jerusalem. "Transport on the Jerusalem road is impossible," was the reply. "You can go to Tel Aviv."

The luggage was being put together in front of what appeared to be a luggage van. There was an underlying sense of portentous gravity attached to every action. I waited expectantly for a bus or a taxi to appear. Then a voice called out: "Take your seats."

Twenty people and luggage were packed together into what I had thought was the luggage van! As the doors were closed and bolted, two small holes securely covered and the lights extinguished, I realised fully that I was in an armoured car, in a country at war. I was setting out on a journey fraught with grave dangers—my way back to Jerusalem!

The darkness within the car was tense; conversation flowed. Questions were asked and answered.

"We have military escort."

"The Arabs are dangerous on this road."

"Two days ago this same driver courageously and miraculously broke through an Arab attack."

"Last week the Arabs succeeded in their attack and all the passengers were killed."

We were driving very slowly with much rattling. The conversation became more intermittent, the atmosphere more tense. It was dark. We could see nothing inside or outside. Sensitiveness to sound increased. The silence within the car was vibrant with anxiety, fear, courage, faith. One hour passed. Suddenly the car stopped; voices were raised.

"Jewish territory!"

"We are safe."

"Thank God!"

The door of the car opened. Light poured in. The tension was relaxed. The engines of the military escort cars were noisily turning back to Lydda.

We continued our journey, passing through lighted streets, increasing our speed, breathing more freely, thanking God for bringing us safely through enemy territory. My first experience of war in the Holy Land!

TEL AVIV

Half an hour later we reached Tel Aviv. I found a room in a hotel. My sleep was disturbed many times during the night by shots and explosions that were not very far away.

The next morning I walked through the streets and was conscious of the shadow of war in the city. Few people were about, the shops were empty, the atmosphere was fraught with unseen dangers. I was about to cross a road not far from the hotel when voices shouted and called out urgently. I turned 'round enquiringly. A few men were beckoning frantically to me.

"Stop!" they cried. "Don't cross that street. Bullets are fired there continually from a mosque in Jaffa. Yesterday a woman risked the crossing—she was killed. Others have been wounded."

"Is it only this street?" I asked.

"Oh no, bullets from Jaffa find their way into all places—even to a child asleep in its bed, or a man at his table in his home. But this particular street is within direct range of the mosque."

"Do the Jews fire back at the mosque?" I asked.

"We do not shoot at mosques or churches," was the reply. The explosion that you heard last night," they said in answer to my question, "was the blowing up of some Arab houses on the Jaffa border, where large quantities of ammunition were stored."

I went to a small café for lunch. I was the only customer. "All our men and women are at military training," explained the owner of the café. "There is no business at all these days."

The sniping went on all day. People in the streets kept near the walls for protection and crossed the roads hurriedly and anxiously.

The sun shone brightly from a very blue sky. The water broke rhythmically upon a deserted beach. The end of the promenade of the Tel Aviv seashore was the beginning of Jaffa. The cluster of houses and mosque towers of that old city bordering the coastline was faintly covered by the haze of the sun and the sea-mist. Behind the sunny haze I saw Joppa, the city of the Bible, Jonah, the ship, the whale—and the return!

Bullets hit a wall very near to where I was standing. It was wiser to keep away from the streets, especially those within range of the minarets.

I wanted to go to Jerusalem. It was impossible. The road to Jerusalem was continually attacked by the Arabs, and all passenger transport was stopped. There had been very serious incidents. The only way open for me was to Haifa.

HAIFA

The following day I left Tel Aviv. The first part of the journey to Haifa was in a taxi, but before entering Arab-occupied territory I had to change into a small armoured car, packed tightly together with five other passengers. We reached Haifa without any encounters. We were fortunate.

I emerged from the inner recess of the armoured car and intended first to visit my friend B.M. to ask for advice about accommodation. I called a taxi and gave the address of a street not far from the centre of the Hadar HaCarmel.

"No," replied the taxi driver, "I won't go there, it is too dangerous. Arab bullets are fired continually into that street." I reconsidered my plan and decided to go to Mount Carmel.

In Haifa the dangers were even greater than in Tel Aviv. The Arab and the Jewish houses were intermingled and bullets came from all directions. Mount Carmel was quieter and very beautiful. I found a room in a peaceful house, and from my window I looked down upon the incredibly lovely picture of Haifa Bay.

SHIPS

In the main street of the Hadar HaCarmel, the Jewish sector of Haifa, the afternoon sun intensified the colours in the shop windows. The streets were filled with people intent upon their business. Faces were serious and thoughtful. A strange, heavy-laden atmosphere mysteriously subdued the bright colourfulness of the scene.

Suddenly a volley of shots was fired from a street nearby and continued intermittently for some minutes. Bullets resounded loudly as they hit stone walls alarmingly close to where I walked. Faces became more serious, the atmosphere more ominous, but the people in the streets and in the shops carried on undisturbed.

I asked a young girl the reason for the shots. "Arabs from nearby houses fire upon us indiscriminately. Let them use up their ammunition; most of the bullets only make holes in the walls," she replied. "We Jews are more careful and save our ammunition for more definite purposes, or for self-defence."

"Most of the bullets only make holes in the walls," she had said, but I was told that some stray bullets found a softer target—a woman out shopping, a child returning from school, a man at work, an infant in bed.

The shooting continued. At a street corner an old man stood in his kiosk selling sweets and fruit drinks. I asked for a drink and after a moment he became very communicative. "My wife and I escaped from Europe, filled with the hope of reaching our own land. Hope of peace! Our son had gone to Palestine before us. We were many months on the way, terrible months!" His thoughts went back. "The hardships on the voyage were unbearable. The last day came. Haifa! We entered the harbour. There were difficulties about landing. The last day seemed longer than the whole voyage!" A shadow of sadness passed over his old face. "Towards evening we left the ship. We searched the faces waiting on the shore. Our son did not meet us! He had been killed that same morning in an accident." The shooting continued in the next street.

On my way back to Mount Carmel the bus was filled with men and women, old and young, their faces tired and strained, hard and determined, resentful, sad, weary.

"Another ship with arms for Palestine has been intercepted," I overheard. "Don't worry," came the reply, "We will get ammunition, we can defend ourselves, the country is ours."

From Mount Carmel I looked down at the bay, the harbour—the gateway to the world. So many ships rested upon the calm blue water; silently, motionlessly. So many ships passed in and out—through the gateway, carrying ammunition, food, oil, human souls.

I opened a newspaper and read: A number of young Jews, men and women, passengers on a ship, were ready to sail for America. A party of Jews boarded the ship and took them off by force. No Jew was allowed to leave the country. Jews in the "Jewish State" were no longer free.

A ship sailed into Haifa Bay. Six hundred illegal immigrants! A British warship steamed alongside. Passengers were transferred and another ship turned its prow toward the horizon, taking its human cargo to Cyprus. Jews were not allowed to land in their own country.

The sunlight made patterns on the blue of the sea, picking out a ship here and there and holding it momentarily in a radiant glow of light. A group of small sailing boats with sails unfurled, a shabby refugee ship, a well-worn cargo ship, an elegant white passenger ship, a grey dignified battleship … The ships of Haifa! What forces control them? What secrets lay hidden beneath their seeming serenity?

An outgoing steamer left a faint trail behind as it made its path into the ocean. Another ship was moving slowly into the harbour. Suddenly a powerful explosion rent the air. My window rattled loudly. As I looked, a huge pillar of smoke rose from the midst of the houses below, not far from the harbour. An Arab house, a military headquarters and an ammunition depot had been destroyed by Jews! Higher and higher the smoke clouds rose until they spread a dark filmy screen across land and sea. Behind the veil the ships of Haifa were almost invisible—grey phantom shapes upon a grey phantom sea.

Beauty, light, warmth, colour, all possibilities, all achievements, hidden behind the screen of grey smoke—the blinding curls of smoke—rising from the flames of destruction.

BULLETS

In a little room in a house on the heights of Mount Carmel I sat together with friends, listening to accounts of their experiences. A neighbour came in with the latest news. "Four Jews waiting for a bus were shot dead by Arabs."

"Where?" I asked.

"Carmel Avenue."

The day before I, too, had been waiting for a bus at the same place! I remembered the uncomfortable feeling I had as I walked down the street to visit friends—one of the few Jewish families still living in the district.

Only Arabs and some British soldiers were to be seen. Barbed wire, armoured cars with guns, and other military vehicles filled the road. I walked along, conscious of all eyes looking upon me with hostile suspicion. Four Jews had been shot dead. I had been lucky.

My thoughts were interrupted as the front door bell rang. A woman was led into the room distraught with anxiety. "My husband has not returned from work," she cried. "Will someone come with me to phone the police?"

She had walked a long way from a village on Mount Carmel where she lived. She was tense with nervous strain and despair. We tried to reassure her. "Perhaps there was a shooting in the streets and he waited at the office. Perhaps he had not been able to get a bus at the usual time. Perhaps …" Two friends accompanied the woman to the nearest telephone.

I went to my room and looked out of the window. The lights of Haifa and the suburbs surrounding the bay were like a shimmering, heavily jeweled necklace encircling the throat of the ocean. In the bay the ships, like clusters of sparkling precious stones, embroidered the darkness together with the stars above.

The lights of Haifa! Arab, Jewish, British, and others! How many of those lights were shining from homes where husbands had not returned from their work? Arabs, Jews, British, and others … In the morning I learned that the woman's husband would never return. He was one of the four killed while waiting for a bus.

The next afternoon I went down to the Hadar HaCarmel to visit my friend B.M. Few people were in the street where he lived. A sign of danger! I arrived safely at my destination and joined the family 'round a table prepared for tea. "We were expecting another friend from Mount Carmel," said B.M., "but we won't wait any longer. Perhaps he is afraid to come. He intended to bring his wife."

Half way through the tea a nearby explosion shook the house. Shots were fired in all directions in the streets outside. Explosions, shots, and more shots. Bullets were whizzing past the window.

Half an hour later there was a pause—it was quiet. I decided to return to Mount Carmel. With hat and coat on, ready to depart, I was delayed a few minutes in conversation. Suddenly the attack started again with renewed intensity. We looked out from the balcony for a few seconds. The shots were coming from number 4. Our house was number 10! Right over my head fiery bullets flashed past.

We closed the windows and lowered the shutters and I decided to wait. Had I not been delayed in conversation I should have been in the street in the midst of the battle—an easy target. We sat 'round the table again, drinking more tea. B.M. spoke about the friend he had expected. "I am sorry he couldn't come," he said, "He was very eager to meet you."

Conversation continued. I picked up a newspaper lying on a chair. "Did you know any of these men?" I asked B.M. handing him the paper. He looked, his face turned pale with shock. "That is my friend," he said, pointing to the first name. "The man I was waiting for. The friend from Mount Carmel."

The shooting continued; it was too dangerous to go out into the streets. I stayed the night at B.M.'s house.

TO JERUSALEM

A man was busy attaching a safety chain to the inner handle of the door of an armoured car. It was the taxi in which I was to travel part of the way to Tel Aviv in route to Jerusalem. I looked questioningly at a number of bullet holes in the sides and back of the car. "Don't worry about that," I was told. "The bullets can't go through." I took my seat behind the driver, in the iron "safe" within the armoured body of the car. I was the only passenger. We started on our journey.

After a few minutes we were out of the Jewish quarter of Haifa. We were driving through "enemy territory." The driver's fingers passed nervously over the safety chain attached to the door. The steel shutters were lowered over the small side windows and wind screen. The roads were precarious with deep ditches on either side. We passed an overturned army lorry [truck] on the way.

Suddenly the heavens seemed to open and a deluge of water flooded the earth. The raindrops covered the small opening through which the world was visible. The driver's fingers passed nervously over the safety chain. The raindrops hardened; hail-stones piled up and obscured visibility. I could see nothing. He drove on. I thought of the overturned army lorry. The car stopped.

"Can't I get out and wipe off the hailstones?" I asked. He looked at me with amused surprise. "It is too dangerous to open the door here. Arabs usually fire at us from this place." I remembered a similar occasion years ago when driving through the wilds of Africa and I was told not to open the door of the car. Lions and other wild animals prowled in that part of the country.

We drove on blindly. It seemed to me there were other dangers besides the Arabs. Suddenly a large dark shape loomed up in the middle of the road. The car pulled up with a jerk, chains and windows rattling. The shape took form—a camel! The tension was relaxed by laughter.

When the storm abated and the road became more visible, I saw another overturned armoured car at the side of the road! The driver's fingers passed nervously over the safety chain. I asked if he had had dangerous experiences with that door. He shrugged his shoulders. His silence was eloquent.

We reached the safety zone. I changed into an open car and said goodbye to the courageous man who had brought me safely through all dangers. He was returning immediately to Haifa. He travelled that road every day—carrying passengers, parcels, mail.

Through Jewish territory toward Tel Aviv we passed Arab villages; Arabs in their homes, in the streets, in the fields. "Peaceful Arabs," I was told. "Under the protection of neighbouring Jewish settlements!" Before the sun set we reached Tel Aviv.

꙾ ꙾

The next morning I waited at the transport office for the car coming in convoy from Jerusalem that was to take passengers back the same day. It was already two hours overdue. Delay on that journey caused anxiety. People went in and out of the office looking expectantly for the awaited car.

"At last!" we called out excitedly. "It is coming."

"Thank God!"—a murmur of relief from someone waiting for a relative.

The grey-painted, steel-covered vehicle stopped at the door, opened its sides and emptied out its human and material contents. The last to be disgorged was a young man—unshaven, haggard, heavy-eyed, slightly unsteady. A sick man, I thought.

After taking a breath, the grey armoured vehicle closed its door again upon its new occupants. With five other human beings and numerous parcels and other articles of luggage, I was packed into the security of its innermost recess. The man at the wheel was the unshaven, haggard, heavy-eyed man I had noticed with concern.

An hour later, hidden in the interior of one of the sixteen grey-painted, steel-covered vehicles, large and small, lined up along the road, I started on my journey to Jerusalem. Leaving the centre of Tel Aviv we passed through some of the poorest suburbs, where all the people, old and young, came out to watch the strange convoy passing through its streets. An old man raised his arms and blessed each car as it went by.

The first part of the way was a deviation from the main road, through the land of the Agricultural School. Men and women working on the land were armed. Windows in buildings were bricked up. Sandbags barricaded doors. They had suffered many attacks from Arabs. The roads were deeply furrowed by torrential rains and unaccustomed heavy traffic. From a small opening I could see the long trailing convoy, looking like some giant mechanical caterpillar divided into many parts, as it swayed and wriggled over the uneven road. Through green fields and desert sands, orange groves and military camps, on and on we rattled and bumped. "Before I do this journey again, I shall have two weeks' practice," came from one of the passengers, sitting grimly between two women and piles of luggage, as we were being helplessly shaken and tossed about.

We passed through villages and settlements; all along were groups of armed guards. I noticed boys and girls aged between twelve and fifteen with rifles hung over their shoulders or revolvers in their belts.

With great relief we approached the main road, where, with increased speed the long grey caterpillar seemed to gather its parts more closely together and to proceed more smoothly on its way. Our driver talked lightly and jokingly. Windows were tightly closed, windscreen shutters lowered. We were passing through a dangerous area, and through the narrow slit of light it was difficult to see anything but the back wheel of the vehicle in front of us. The driver's haggard face twitched nervously; his eyes were heavy-lidded. The air was hot and stifling. In each of the sixteen parts of that moving train there was a man at the wheel, a man who risked his life daily, whose nerves were strained to the utmost by the difficulties of the journey, whose courage and endurance made the life-line of transport possible. People on different missions, food-stuffs, necessary commodities of life and equipment for all purposes moved along this life-line. Without this means of transport, life in the cities could not go on. Brave men willingly offered their lives daily, and in some of those grey vehicles were young men and women, boys and girls, armed and watchful, who protected the convoy and repulsed many attacks. So many of these young lives had already been sacrificed to make this journey possible.

We left the plains and climbed the winding road through the hills of Judea. Slowly, carefully, guardedly, we passed through Arab villages, Arab military camps, hiding places from which the enemy fired almost daily. There were no incidents that day. At other times mines had been exploded on the road, people had been killed—murdered.

Through the less dangerous parts of the way the shutter was slightly raised. Heavy masses of cloud were illuminated by the red rays of the setting sun, casting shadows upon the splendour of the hills. The hills of Judea! Visible only through an inch-wide slit in an armoured car—the road to Jerusalem. My fellow passengers were silent. Their faces showed signs of anxiety, discomfort, tension, and fatigue. It was difficult for them to return a friendly smile. The face of the driver twitched nervously.

On a hill two figures were silhouetted against the sky. The windows were opened; the front shutter was lifted. The men on the hill waved as we passed. "Now we are safe," said the driver. "Jewish territory!"

Ten minutes later we extricated ourselves from the luggage. With aching head and cramped limbs I stepped out of the car. I thanked God for bringing us safely through all dangers. I looked at the nervous, tense faces 'round me. Jerusalem.

CHAPTER SEVEN

NIGHT

MARCH–JULY, 1948

March 8, 1948! I had reached the end of my journey; I had made my way back to Jerusalem! The events foreshadowed by the picture I had taken away with me on my departure in 1946 had developed into the reality of the present. All Jewish life was now compressed into a small area, the centre of which was reduced to ruins and wreckage, extending through many streets leading out of Ben Yehuda Street.

THE BATTERED CITY

My first visit was to a friend living on one of those streets near Ben Yehuda Street. I had difficulty in reaching the entrance of the building—stepping over broken glass, stones, twisted iron, shattered pieces of wood, and other rubble piled outside. On the stairs were the same signs of destruction. I did not expect to find my friend.

The door of the flat was half torn away. I stepped in and called. My friend Pearl looked up from the chaos that she was trying to restore to order. She was astonished to see me. I was glad to see that she was unhurt. "Ten days ago this happened," she said. "I have been staying with friends until today; my nerves were so shaken, I couldn't even come back to see what had happened to my home."

All the windows and doors were broken, ceilings and walls were cracked, furniture was destroyed. She took me into one room where the whole wall had collapsed. It was her daughter's bedroom. "Nora's bed was against that wall," she said. "On the morning of the explosion she was on early duty at her work. She left home at six o'clock. Half an hour later her bed was beneath this debris."

"And you?" I asked.

"I was alone in the flat," she replied, taking me to her room, which was the least damaged. "I was awakened from my sleep by the explosion, not knowing what had happened. Broken glass, clouds of dust in the room, and I lay stunned, unable to move. Cries and screams came from the neighbours. Then someone came in and helped me up."

I went out on the balcony from where I could see the corner of Ben Yehuda Street. "It was just there," said Pearl, pointing to the devastated building, "that two British army lorries, filled with explosives, were left to do their work."

"My brother, who lives 'round the corner, saw the lorries arrive. He was curious and went out into the street to look. He saw men in uniform leave the lorries and drive away in a car. He was a little suspicious and hurried back to his home. The shattering explosion rocked the city before he could reach his door. He is in the hospital, but is very lucky—only his leg is hurt."

"Didn't you have friends living in Ben Yehuda Street?" I asked Pearl. "At that corner," she answered, "where the building is completely demolished, there was a block of flats. My friend, her husband and two children lived there. They are all dead! And so many others—men, women, and children!" The tears filled her eyes; her nerves were still very shaken.

Piles of wreckage and rubble filled many streets. Workmen were busy repairing walls and windows wherever repair was possible. Men and women were clearing the debris of shattered shops. Wherever a small space was cleared, they carried on bravely with their business, selling their goods, salvaged or newly acquired, supplying the needs of the people.

All the streets were barricaded and guarded. Stone walls, bricks, iron bars, sandbags, barbed wire! It was difficult to walk through any streets other than the main roads kept clear for traffic. Wherever I walked, I came to the end of the road—strong barricades and many armed soldiers—indicating clearly that beyond the barrier was another zone—Arab or British, or Arab and British combined.

Any person passing from one zone to another risked his life. There were certain areas of no-man's land between two zones, but even there the dangers were great. There were daily encounters with the enemy, and in all circles one heard of the loss of courageous and recklessly daring young people.

IN THE THROES

On the morning of March 11th I walked along King George Avenue, but soon came to a heavily barricaded street block, guarded by a number of armed British soldiers. It was the entrance to the British security zone. At the border I stood for a few moments, looking at the Jewish Agency Building. I wondered how long it would remain intact! I turned to walk back. Children were playing in a nearby garden, babies asleep in their carriages.

A few minutes later an explosion rent the air and shook the earth. For a moment I was paralyzed with shock. A huge column of smoke and dust was rising from the places I had just left. After a moment of suspended life, streams of humanity poured out from all the buildings into the streets, as if drawn by a magnet, rushing toward the vicinity of the explosion. The atmosphere was charged with a sense of calamity.

The overstrained nerves of a people living constantly under the shadow of death were severely tried. Women wept, men's faces were pale. Cars raced through the streets, hooting loudly and urgently, all the traffic flying toward the scene of disaster.

Before long some of the motor traffic was on its return journey to first-aid posts and hospitals. I saw wounded, blood-stained men and women, in cars, on stretchers, conscious and unconscious.

Backward and forward raced the cars, the ambulances, the people. Questions were being asked in the street, opinions were being exchanged.

"The Jewish Agency building!"

"How is it possible?"

"The streets are so guarded!"

"British help!"

"This is the work of the Arabs!"

"Many killed and wounded!"

Some British army lorries passed through the streets carrying soldiers. Guns were pointed toward the people. The atmosphere was tense. Only three weeks before, British army lorries had entered Ben Yehuda Street.

On my way to my room I passed the square in Ben Yehuda Street, a square where buildings had been reduced to a mass of wreckage and surrounding houses stood like grim skeletons, their naked frames exposed. This square is now known by a new name, an English name—Bevin Square. In Tel Aviv, the all-Jewish city of Palestine, built up within the past twenty years, the main street is named Allenby Street, the main square, Balfour Square—all English names. A tribute to England and the spirit of Englishmen, whose help made the creation of that city possible.

A SABBATH DAY

I was awakened at dawn by a strange medley of sounds. The voice of a man singing, calling out in prayer to his Creator. The loud reports of guns accompanied his prayers. I opened the shutters of my window and the first rays of the morning sun, spreading a misty glow over the city, entered my room and filled it with light. From the roof of a torn and twisted building came the joyful song of birds—it was spring! Gunfire, prayers, bird-song! A Sabbath morning in the Holy City! Destruction, faith, hope!

There were many who filled the synagogues to pray; many who beat their breasts and sang prayers of lamentation and supplication; many who shed tears of anguish and despair; parents who wept for their children—those children behind the guns whose shooting accompanied the chanting of their elders.

At midday it was quiet again; the sun was shining brightly. The shops were closed. The streets were filled with men and women, resting from the labours of the week. The children were playing in the streets, in the gardens, in the squares. I walked through the streets wherever it was possible to walk, the "safety area" was very restricted. I ventured to the end of a road from which I could see the hills, risking the danger of sniping from those very hills. I longed to see, just for a moment, a different picture from that which had been before me ever since I had arrived in Jerusalem— rubble, wreckage, barricades, distress.

The silvery green shapes of the distant olive trees and warm-tinted sandy paths around the hills accentuated the soft colours of the hills. Nearby was an almond tree in blossom, its tender beauty full of the fresh hope of spring. Delicate clouds floating across a very blue sky seemed to capture some of the rosy flush of the flower petals. I drank deeply of all that beauty, a reminder that the work of God was still visible on the earth.

I turned my steps back to the "safety area." A volley of shots broke in upon my thoughts: machine guns, mortars—loud, frequent, and urgent. The shots were fired into the heart of the city. The crowds in the streets ran to take shelter; children screamed and bent low on the ground. Some streets could not be crossed. The firing was incessant and dangerous. I could not return to my room, the shots were being fired into the surrounding streets. I took refuge in the entrance of a building, together with many others. For half an hour there was no pause. Then I took advantage of a quiet interval to run across the danger area and finally reached my room.

It was now the end of the Sabbath day. The shooting continued, noisily and treacherously. The sun had disappeared behind the hills; darkness covered the crimes that were being perpetrated. I carried within my heart the memory of the soft tinted hills, the blue sky, the tender almond blossom. And I looked into the future with the hope that a Sabbath day would dawn when bird song and the voice of mankind would be mingled together, singing in praise and thanksgiving; when the sound of shooting would no longer be heard in the Holy City nor in any other part of the world.

STREET SCENES

In an atmosphere of war and danger human emotions become abnormally tense. Like dried straw that can be set alight by the merest spark, the people of Jerusalem were keyed up and easy targets for the fiery darts that blew with every breeze in that distressed city.

Walking out one morning from the place where I lived, in the centre of the city, I passed a long queue of harassed but hopeful women; well dressed women, women in rags, cultured women, peasant women; each one with an empty shopping bag or piece of wrapping paper. The queue began at a fish shop which had not opened its doors for weeks. It was still not open, but the previous day a convoy had come through from Tel Aviv with food supplies, the first for several weeks. There was some hope, it was still early in the day.

Further along the street was another queue waiting for a door to open—bread! And still another queue of pregnant women, and women with young children—perhaps they would get a little milk. I passed a restaurant where occasionally I had enjoyed a good vegetarian meal. It was closed. At a kiosk where I usually had a drink of orange juice, the proprietor could only supply some brown watery mixture and a few odd sweets.

I walked on. A little later my attention was attracted by the sudden rush of the people in the street toward an excited crowd gathering in the next street. I was curious. There had been no explosion. What could it be? There was shouting and excitement. I saw the looks of enquiry and in some faces curiosity, anxiety, fear. In the midst of the excited crowds were two lorries. I asked what was happening. "They have taken some Arab prisoners from a nearby village and are transferring them to another lorry."

I walked on toward Rehavia, hoping for a glimpse of some open space. There was sniping in the area but one hardly noticed that. Along King George Avenue there was a garden where I had seen the anemones in bud, and I anticipated the joy of the flowers in full bloom. Now a high wall had been built, a battlement, which safeguarded the passers-by from the shots coming across the garden. The beauty of the opened anemone buds blossomed unseen.

As I was nearing the barrier, a car stopped at the side of the road, and suddenly, with frantic waving of hands and shouts from the guards, people ran away in all directions. I was persuaded to run too, and then discovered the reason for the flight. A car had come in with a box of oranges and it was suspected that there was a bomb in the box. All the streets in the vicinity were cleared. Later I learned that a time-bomb had been found and removed in time.

I decided to leave the streets for a while and to visit a friend. I entered the home of a peaceful, cultured family. A woman was in tears. "My son," she said, "was killed last night." I looked at the photo standing on a table—a boy of twenty, a fine intelligent face; a brilliant scholar, a devoted son. A young girl was trying to console her mother. She had returned from the fight in which her brother had been killed.

A university professor had told me that his students were all disappearing. His classes were smaller each day. The sound of guns and mortar explosions not very far off added to the pathos of the situation. One could not escape from the desolation of the streets even inside the home!

A woman came in very troubled about her daughter, who was due to give birth to a child. An operation was necessary. A convoy had left that morning for the Hadassah Hospital, taking doctors, nurses, medical supplies, hospital staff, and invalids. The woman was thankful that they had taken her daughter.

The sound of heavy gunfire continued. I returned to my room burdened by all I had seen and heard. I passed the queue still waiting at the fish shop. It had lengthened considerably. Nerves were strained; patience was wearing out. I could see no fish. I was told they would only get their numbers that day and would have to queue again the next day for the fish.

In the middle of the road a large lorry-borne water tank was drawing people toward it from all the houses. Buckets, jugs, tins, every available utensil was brought out to be filled with water. The water supply was running low.

Shooting in the surrounding neighbourhood continued. A fierce battle was in progress. What was happening?

Some hours later I learned that the battle had been on Mount Scopus—on the road to the Hadassah Hospital. The Arabs had attacked the convoy on its way there. Over seventy Jews had been killed and many wounded—doctors, nurses, invalids. The woman's daughter and her unborn child had been murdered. The seeds of war bear bitter fruit.

TRAVAIL: 14 MAY, 1948

With the obvious signs of the infant state in the womb of Israel nearing its time of delivery, a hostile world schemed to bring about a pre-natal destruction, or at least to cripple the life that would not be destroyed.

The Jewish right to freedom in the land of Israel could not be denied, but it would be restricted freedom in a partitioned land; a divided state, where the neighbour state could be used as a mask for the hostile world.

With the acceptance of partition, the labour pains commenced. The Jewish State was about to be born! The painful travail of the past six months was in the final stage preceding birth.

It was the last day of the British Mandate. British military forces were evacuating their security zone in Jerusalem. All the government officials were ready to leave. The High Commissioner bade farewell to Jerusalem over the radio.

The Sabbath eve! The shooting died down. All through the night the imminent event cast an awed silence over the city. Jerusalem waited breathlessly.

BIRTH: 15 MAY, 1948

The pre-natal pains are over! Amidst bloodshed, suffering, and anguish, in an atmosphere of hostility, the Jewish State is born. It is named: "The State of Israel" and is destined to withstand all its enemies. It is born a partitioned land, not yet receiving the full blood-stream from its throbbing heart—Jerusalem!

The frustrated world is compelled to accept the partitioned State—the body. But Jerusalem—the heart, the soul—is the seat of the battle.

On this momentous day of birth—the Sabbath day—I write from the city of Jerusalem, the Jewish city, the Holy City. The palpitating heartbeats, throbbing with life's destiny, can be felt in all people, in all places, at all times.

In the morning the hushed silence continued, charged with suppressed excitement, fearful expectancy, anxiety-veiled joy. The streets are emptier than usual. Small groups of people gather anxiously and curiously at corners near the entrance to "Bevingrad," the evacuated British security zone. Later the Jewish flag is hoisted on the "General Building," which has housed the British police. Only an occasional shot is heard in the distance.

The silence is tense; the people wait for the proclamation of birth. No newspapers! No electricity! No radio broadcast! Undercurrents of suppressed joy and fear flow through the city in alternate waves.

What is happening to the new-born life? Will it be allowed to take breath? Will the world accept it? Are the enemies' fingers 'round its throat intending to strangle it? The heartbeats are loud and fast in the Jewish city of Jerusalem.

Before long the silence is broken; the awe of birth is over. The guns, silenced momentarily by the powers turning the page of destiny, open fire and volleys of shots are poured into the throbbing heart of Israel's city.

Moslems, aided by "Christians," are attacking the Jews from Mount Zion.

STRUGGLE FOR LIFE: 18 MAY, 1948

It is two days since the birth of the State of Israel. An aftermath of pain, anguish, fear, and bloodshed; of courage, sacrifice, and faith; of chained freedom and obscured joy.

The enemy surrounds us—is on our doorstep! Terrible battles are in progress. All sections of the Jewish city are being shelled. Heavy explosions continually rend the air, leaving behind a trail of destruction, death, pain, and shattered nerves. Helpless men, women, and children are being injured and killed. Shops are closed, streets are cleared. Jerusalem is a desolate city: no food, no water supply, no lighting, no news broadcasts. All able men and women are called up for full-time service. The enemy is pushing at the door.

Jerusalem is like a city under sentence of death, bearing within it the certainty of life. The heart of Israel cannot be destroyed. Death in the Holy City can only mean resurrection—new life.

20 MAY, 1948

A deathly pallor still rests on the face of Jerusalem. From midnight to dawn the cannons roared, shells exploded, machine guns rattled, and every other type of gun added to the infernal noise that penetrated every house in the city. The sleepless, helpless inhabitants listened in tense silence and darkness to the battle of life and death.

With the first rays of dawn, the birds made a brave effort to counteract the nerve-racking sounds of continuous battle. The light of day brought with it the relief of abated shooting and shelling, followed by a period of comparative quiet.

I went out to get some news. The *Palestine Post*—for the first time in its history—could not be printed. We received a few stenciled pages. News passed from mouth to mouth.

"Mount Zion is in Jewish hands!"

"Our flag flies on the Tower of David!"

"The Haganah have joined up with the defenders within the Old City!"

Fifteen hundred Jews had held their positions for many days against thirty thousand Arabs within the walls of the Old City! Last night a handful of Jews penetrated the massive ramparts surrounding the city and brought relief to the brave defenders within. News items continued to be passed on.

"Reinforcements of troops, guns, and tanks are pouring in for the Arab Legion."

"Amongst the captured Arab prisoners are British officers."

Bullets and shells whiz past overhead as I write, exploding at all distances, near and far. Women and children strained with fear, anxiety, lack of food and water, and many sleepless, terrifying nights, seek safe places of shelter.

Darkness is now awaiting the departure of the sun. It is symbolic that Jerusalem is at this time without light. In the utter darkness of this life and death struggle, the light of prayer is making a trail in the heart of mankind. There is much prayer opening the way to God in this tormented city. It will need more prayer and more dependence upon the God of Israel before the State of Israel can come into its full inheritance.

The struggle for the new life continues; the shadows are darkening. What has this night in store for us?

"Yea, though I walk through the valley of the shadow of death, I will fear no evil; for thou art with me: thy rod and thy staff they comfort me."

EXTRACTS FROM LETTERS

(Letters that were written but could not be posted for three months, all postal communications being cut off.)

11 MAY, 1948

For two days there has been silence; such a strange silence after the fierce battles fought on our doorsteps recently. It is almost an uncanny silence, especially as these last few days are fraught with a tension poised between the death of the British Mandatory Power and the birth of the Jewish State!

There are many vital decisions pending, vital at least for the daily life of Jerusalem. The road to Tel Aviv has been blocked for several weeks, which means, of course, no supplies … In Jerusalem there are preparations going on for the worst—fortifications are being strengthened, air-raid shelters built, all man-power called up for full-time service. The Jews have learned through bitter experience not to trust anyone or anything. We are preparing for the worst and hoping for the best!

There is very little food, very little water, very little electricity. Our rations are a quarter of a loaf of bread per day, and very occasionally a spoonful of jam or an ounce of cheese.

The recent Jerusalem battles were fought on the border of the suburb where I live, so for a few days and nights it was not so quiet! A bullet piercing the cushion on which he was sleeping awakened a neighbour retiring on Saturday afternoon. Another neighbour lost the soup she was preparing for lunch when a bullet went through the saucepan. I just missed a bullet in the street when returning home one day, but another woman just before me was not so fortunate—she was killed!

I must find a ration of water for the day, which must be as little as possible, until the water pipes are repaired and Jerusalem can be supplied again. Many nights I have to go to bed at sundown (about 7:30) because there is no electricity, no candles, no fuel of any kind. But the Jews are used to suffering and bear it all so wonderfully. It really is very moving to see how courageously they carry on in spite of all difficulties.

The Jewish population here is confident of the victory of their Jewish State, but they are prepared for the need to make still greater sacrifices. They are no longer deluded by any apparently friendly gesture from the outside world.

10 JUNE, 1948

There have been so many changes in Jerusalem since I came. The material life has become more and more difficult each day. Less and less food, water, heating, and light. The physical dangers have increased daily. Intermittent shooting has developed into fierce battles day and night—battles for the life of Jerusalem. Bullets in the streets gave way to shells, mortar bombs, incendiaries and other deadly missiles. The darkness of destruction and terror came upon us all with ever increasing fury.

The Jewish people are feeling more and more that God is with them. The Bible is read and quoted in every place: in the camps of the young people, in the fighting line, in the hospitals, in the refugee houses, in homes and other places where previously it was ignored or even ridiculed. A new light is beginning to burn—however small it may be—in the terrible darkness of these days.

The bombardment of shells and mortar bombs goes on day and night; every sector of Jewish Jerusalem gets it in turn. At night I lie in my bed, alone in a small single-storied house, the occupants of which are in a shelter—and I count the explosions around me—though I have not often been afraid. The remarkable thing is that although we have so many sleepless nights, so little food, so many difficulties in every way, so much continued nervous strain—the people can carry on calmly and with such strength. I feel indeed that God's protecting spirit is at work. I have felt it in myself and I see it in all the people around me, as a power to withstand all without any undue reaction. And each day the onslaught comes with greater fury, and the rations get smaller and smaller.

Although there have been days when there was hardly an interval between the shelling, and all were hidden in shelters or the inner rooms of their homes, there has not been one day that I missed going from my room to Pearl's flat. It was not recklessness; neither was it bravado or defiance. But I felt a quiet conviction that I should go each day, and so I walked very calmly and quietly through the streets, and I was glad to have the experience of being on the open battlefield and in contact with the wounded city at the moment it was being hit. Some days it seemed as if I was the only living being in Jerusalem—there was no other person to be seen. Each day as I walked along my route I saw new shell holes, new damage, new wreckage. Some days I followed a trail of shells—the bloodstains were still fresh on the pavement. The human victims had been removed, but the body of a horse still lay at the side of the road and a little dog in the middle of the road. The damaged cars and other vehicles added to the desolation of the scene.

In Ben Yehuda Street a shell fell on the pavement outside a small restaurant where people were at breakfast—several were killed and wounded. It had made a hole in the place where an old man usually sat with his "shoe shine" outfit. The bloodstains on the pavement were hardly dry, but the old man had found a sheet of iron to cover up the shell hole, and he was arranging his "shoe shine" outfit in his usual place.

But it is at the hospitals that the tragedy hits one hardest. A nurse from a hospital said to me: "It gets worse daily. From this hospital alone we bury about thirty people every day. We can only take those who are very badly wounded, we have no room for the others."

There are many hospitals like that, and the wounded and dead are the old men, the women, and the children: peaceful Jewish citizens of Jerusalem, brave people attending to their duties— buying bread, getting water, doing essential work. My neighbour, a young woman, went daily to her work in the centre of the town. Two days ago I went a little way with her and then turned back, as I still had something to do before I could leave my room. Half an hour later I heard that she had been wounded by a shell. She will probably lose her leg.

In every house, in every family, there is a victim of this infernal attack. People collect fragments of shells and unexploded bombs—they are all British made.

To be here, to see the restraint, the wisdom, and the tolerance of the Jews; to see the spirit in which they take all this attack, the eagerness and readiness to stop this destruction and make peace, the way in which they meet each new situation, their quiet strength and faith—I can only say that I am so proud and so happy to belong to this people, so happy and so thankful to be here in Jerusalem at this time. It is indeed a great privilege.

When I go out each day trying to find some food and get the rations for my neighbour, and when the ration is only two slices of bread for the day—nothing else—and some days not even that, I wonder still more at the endurance and strength of the people. Then I see how God is with me all the time, because always, in some unforeseen way, food comes to me from different sources. All I do is to go quietly on my way each day, and what is necessary is given to me—for all my needs and also for the needs of others for whom I feel responsible. I am also given the opportunity to help with words of peace, when fear and panic overtake some people. I am always filled with such peace and calm, even when faced with blood and suffering, that it amazes me and fills me with continual wonder and thanksgiving.

Sometimes the electricity comes on for an hour or so at about three in the morning. I start immediately to boil some water for drinking, wash and iron my clothes, and drink as many cups of tea as I can, to make up for the days when I can't get a hot drink! It is wonderful how one can adjust oneself to all conditions of life.

The water-cart comes 'round nearly every day and we get our ration—a bucketful of water. It is interesting to see how much can be done with it! It is more wonderful to see how these brave men come through the shells to deliver the water; some days it is so bad that people prefer to be without water rather than go out into the streets to get it.

In addition to all the other war conditions we now have air-raids—which means the blackout and the warnings of the sirens. Last night a bomb that was dropped from the air exploded in the next street—a reminder of war days in London!

When the infernal noise of the night dies down in the morning and people come out of the shelters, I hear the notes of a Chopin étude. The little girl next door never misses her half-hour practice on the piano.

11 JUNE, 1948

This morning there is to be the cease-fire! Nobody trusts it. Yesterday there was to be a cease-fire in Jerusalem for four hours to allow the Red Cross to move. Everyone was out in the streets; women were doing their shopping, pushing their baby carriages, men were queuing for one cigarette, people were trying to clear the debris. One felt the passionate desire in everyone for peace, and the opportunity to go on with a constructive life—the Arabs took advantage. The bombardment started after a short time. Many were killed … Last night it continued. A terrible battle went on during the early hours of the morning. The Arabs attacked with full force, trying to do as much damage as possible before today's four-week cease-fire. Nobody is very happy about the cease-fire, even though so longing for peace. The terms are so much against us and so much in favour of the Arabs. What will be the end of the four weeks?

16 JUNE, 1948

Now we have "peace"! It is a very shadowed peace, but it is good to see people out in the streets again trying to live a "normal" life after being shut inside their houses and shelters for so many weeks while the terror reigned in the city. It is good to sleep at night without being disturbed by the infernal noise of guns and shells. It is good to be able to walk a little without the danger of death at every step!

And now we wait hopefully for some extra food supplies to come in, and perhaps more water, and some electricity.

3 JULY, 1948

The first news we look for in the newspapers, or ask of those who may have any information, is about the road—the road to Tel Aviv, the life-line of the city. The enemy also concentrates upon the road.

Hard battles are fought there day and night. No convoy can get through. The water-pipe line has been blown up. How long will our supplies in Jerusalem last?

There are secret whispers of a new road being built! Nobody speaks about it. But a fresh hope filters through the fears of threatened dangers.

6 JULY, 1948

Today there is great excitement in Zion Square. Several lorries have arrived with foodstuffs! Everybody is asking, "How did they get through?" "Is it the new road?" We dared to believe the rumours. A convoy had come through! It means life.

However, in the hospitals the tragedy cannot be forgotten. I go to one every day now to help. The sights I see are indescribable. Men, women, and little children—limbs crushed, torn, and mutilated; bodies wounded, eyes blinded, helpless old men and women, unable to understand what has happened to them; innocent young children without arms and legs—or even worse—such pain and suffering.

All things here are more difficult these days. Imagine the conditions in the overcrowded hospitals, the terrible heat of the *chamsin*, the hot desert wind, no water, not enough supplies. It is wonderful how they really do manage in these circumstances … Join me in thanksgiving for all the protection that I have had, and also our friends, through all the dark and dangerous days …

25 JULY, 1948

I think the war period is over in Jerusalem and we have started on the "peace" period. We still have some shots and shells to remind us of what we have just come through, and the bath still serves for purposes other that what it was intended for; candle ends are still very precious and clean clothes a luxury—but still there is peace, and hope for a greater measure of peace in the near future. There are plums sold freely in the streets and potatoes can be had without the ration book; so indeed we are very well off.

NEWS FROM THE OUTSIDE

A knock at the door! A telegram for me! A cable from Heston Farm—the first communication from the outside world for nearly three months! My neighbours share the excitement and joy with me. It is again possible to send and receive messages to and from anxious relatives and friends outside Jerusalem!

Some days later letters arrived by a special "taxi" post. Then came the first food parcels. The following weeks Jerusalem was a city of parcels. They were piled up on the pavement outside the transport offices, and nearly every man, woman, and child in the streets was carrying a parcel or two under their arms.

CHAPTER EIGHT

FLAMES

JULY–AUGUST, 1948

A Sabbath morning. The Old City is in flames! Smoke is rising from the burning synagogues within its walls! Driven out of their burning homes, after months of attack, hunger and thirst, those brave Jewish people: men, women, and children—a mere handful in comparison with the numbers of the enemy—have been forced to surrender. For many months they had defended their homes, their synagogues, their lives. With little ammunition, cut off from all supplies of arms and food, from all communication with their brethren outside the walls, their power to hold out so long cannot be explained in term of this world.

THE OLD CITY

The flames are rising from the Old City! I remember my visit there three years ago: the narrow winding cobbled streets, the primitive homes, the men and boys with their tight knee-breeches, long dark coats, skull caps, and side curls; the old Jews in their richly coloured silk coats and fur-trimmed hats.

I remember the Sabbath days with all the preparations beforehand—cooking, cleaning, washing; the synagogues filled with voices in prayer: so many synagogues, ancient and new—so many prayers ascending from the people of Israel to their God!

I remember being led through intricate passages, up and down stone steps, to synagogues ancient with tradition and treasures, their walls imbued with the hope and cry of Israel throughout the centuries; also synagogues comparatively new, which took up the echoes of the past, reviving and repeating them. I remember being allowed to peep through a hole in the door of a small room with cushioned benches 'round its walls and carpeted floor, a place of strong spiritual power and mystery. Men prayed there silently for hours, at the merging of night and day—a Kabbalist synagogue. Now the flames are leaping! All the synagogues are burning!

I remember the Wailing Wall, where Jewish men and women poured out their petitions and sorrows to the stones that surrounded the Temple of their forefathers—believing that the stones have power to make their prayers heard by God. I remember the brick wall that had been built a few yards from the Wailing Wall and the British sentry on guard while the Jews were at prayer. So many had been shot or stabbed in the back by the Arabs while their faces were turned to the wall—in the outpouring of their hearts to God.

The flames illumined my memories. I recalled the eve of the Passover festival—my first Passover in the Holy Land—when I was invited for the seder to a home in the Old City. Passing through the narrow streets, with occasional glimpses into primitive homes, where tables were prepared for the feast—I arrived at my destination.

An arched doorway, a cobbled courtyard, up a few stone steps, and then a surprising and unexpected atmosphere of beauty and artistic refinement transforming the squalid, primitive surroundings, without detracting from the fascination of their character. From a terrace decked with flowering plants I entered a small room where the mystery of the Old City of Jerusalem and western culture were harmoniously united.

The arched ceiling and small windows looking out on the irregular roofs and walls gave an atmosphere that remained riveted in one's consciousness, even when one's attention was drawn to the festive table—the fine embroidered linen, the silver, glass and china, the flowers, the candles, the *matzoth*.

It was the home of the former Chief Rabbi of Warsaw—a very respected and learned old man—and his wife and family, who had escaped from the Nazis in Poland in a miraculous way and had come as refugees to Jerusalem.

We sat 'round the table prepared for the festival Passover. The old rabbi in his spotless white robe sat upon a large white cushion at the head of the table; on his head his fur-rimmed hat, and beneath the ring of rich brown fur the blue eyes, the delicate skin and the long white beard conjured up in one's mind the pictures of our prophets and forefathers of old.

Beside him sat his wife, a frail woman with finely chiselled face of delicate beauty; eyes sad with suffering and alive with warm friendliness. The black lace veil over her grey-haired wig framed her face like a cameo. A son, his wife and child, a daughter, a granddaughter, several friends, and the circle 'round the table was closed.

The ceremony began. The story of the exodus from Egypt was read, relating the miracles God had performed as he brought his people Israel out of bondage, on the way to the promised land. Moses could only see the promised land from the distance. We were actually sitting in the place where the first Temple was built! We were *in* the promised land. I looked through the window—Jerusalem.

All those 'round the table had come from different lands—Poland, England, Russia, South Africa, Germany. Miracles had brought the people of Israel out of Egypt. Miracles had brought each one of us together 'round that table in the Old City. We read of the enemies in Egypt at the time of Moses—of the enemies in the promised land. We felt the similarity of our position today: enemies in every country, enemies in our own land. We read of the fate of the enemy who had tried to withstand the power of God. The Jewish people were led out of Egypt—they are now being led out of all countries of the world. God's promises to Israel are always fulfilled.

The meal was over, the readings and prayers were finished. The old rabbi withdrew. I talked to the *Rebbitzen* (rabbi's wife) and her daughter Malla. I heard how they had suffered and escaped from the Nazis. How they managed to save some of their belongings and two particularly precious possessions: a treasured priceless Tanach (Old Testament) belonging to the rabbi, and an oil portrait of a beautiful young daughter who had died before they left Poland. I saw the tears always threatening to overflow the eyes of the *Rebbitzen*.

Three years have passed! Now I see the flames rising from that home from which Malla had rescued her old and ailing parents at the beginning of the Siege of the Old City. Again they had escaped with their lives, snatched out of the hands of their enemies, this time without any possessions.

UPROOTED

As I was recalling in my mind these pictures of the Old City as I had seen them on my previous visit, there was a knock on my door. My friend Malla, the rabbi's daughter, came in, looking very pale and distressed. She took my hand.

"The women and children are being escorted out of the Old City today," she said. "Come with me to help in receiving them."

It was only ten minutes' walk to Kiryath Shmuel, the suburb where many beautiful houses had been abandoned by the Arabs after battles during the previous weeks. In these empty houses refugees were being lodged. Crowded together, sitting on the floor, all earthly possessions tied in a bundle beside them, were old men and women; rabbis who had spent their lives in the now smouldering synagogues of the Old City; women who knew nothing of the world beyond the homes in which they had served their husbands and families. Their primitive lives, lived in the tradition of centuries, was expressed in their faces.

They were now uprooted from their world, unable to grasp the meaning of the calamity that had befallen them. Some wept in despair; others were resigned—praying silently, while a few shouted hysterically in anger and bitterness. Then there were the younger women, and the sad faces of children with fear in their eyes, and thin half-starved bodies. Young mothers held babies in their arms. Signs of suffering were on all faces. In the streets more were arriving—old men and women. The Arabs held the young men as prisoners. It was a very hot day. The refugees carried their tins, begging for a drink. There was no water.

An old woman saw Malla and fell at her feet weeping. She had been a neighbour of theirs in the Old City. Words were difficult between them.

"Everything has gone," the woman muttered between her sobs. "At first they came into our houses and shot at us. Then, as they set fire to our homes, we retreated. We hid for days in cellars and kept alive with a little food we had stored. When they came to burn the last houses, we had to surrender."

"And our home?" asked Malla, her last hope dying. For a moment the old woman could not answer, then she cried: "I saw it burning with my own eyes."

I remembered again the portrait of Malla's sister, who died in Poland—her mother's most precious possession; the old rabbi's Tanach, which he valued above all things, and which even the Nazis had permitted him to take with him. I remembered the different things that had been collected together to make that home in the Old City. What the Nazis had permitted them to take out of their Polish home the Arabs had destroyed in their home in Jerusalem!

I looked at Malla. She was very pale and very brave. "They can destroy our possessions and burn our homes," she said. "But we will build new ones. They cannot take our land from us. We are in Israel."

There were shouts and people were running to the end of the dusty road—the water-cart had arrived! Each one received a small ration of water. Later the bread arrived and was cut into measured chunks. There was nothing else that day. The next day there was hot soup, a little margarine, and some black olives.

Smoke was still rising from the burning synagogues and homes in the Old City. The flames had done their work.

❧ ❧

TERRORISTS

During the first weeks after my arrival in Jerusalem, at the beginning of March, I lived in the centre of the Jewish Zone. I was then very conscious of the powers directing the radical and more violent elements within the Jewish people. There were always groups of armed soldiers in and around certain cafés in the neighbourhood. There was an atmosphere of secrecy, an expression of emotions fired by hatred and ruthlessness—a determination to crush the enemy by any means; fiery emotions often leading blindly to mistaken deeds that rebounded upon the whole Jewish people. "These are meeting places of two terrorist groups—'Irgun' and 'Stern,'" I was told. "The worst deeds were conceived and executed by members of the Stern group."

During the three difficult months of siege, which bound the people of Jerusalem together by common danger and suffering and linked them to the city of Jerusalem by all the links of thousands of years, reawakened from the depths of the subconscious to a new consciousness, these darker elements seemed to decrease in power. However, they were still at work, as I was to learn from experience.

Arriving one day in August at a flat of my friend Pearl on my usual daily visit, I found her looking very disturbed. "Three men and a woman called half an hour ago, questioning me about you and other friends," she said. "They will call again today to see you. I didn't like the look of them," she said, with a very worried expression on her face.

Before she could say any more there was a ring at the door. Two men and a girl in uniform and one man in civilian clothes entered the room, bringing with them an atmosphere that accelerated the speed of my heartbeats.

They asked me very politely if I could tell them anything about Mrs. H.—a friend of mine whom they suspected of having dealings with the Arabs and British. I laughed. "She is a good religious woman who has lived in Jerusalem for many years; she has many friends among the Arabs and British. The idea of her being a spy or traitor to Israel is ridiculous."

They asked me about others whom I knew, and some of whom I had never heard. Then they asked Pearl and me to accompany them to their office, as we might be able to help them. I felt the fear behind Pearl's calmness and, although a little unsteady myself, we both went quietly and amiably out of the flat with our escort of four.

A car was waiting for us in the street. Conversation was polite and friendly. As we reached the outskirts of the town handkerchiefs were tied 'round our heads—we were blindfolded. We drove on for about twenty minutes, then we were helped out of the car and guided carefully along stony paths and down the difficult descent of a hill until we reached the steps of a house.

Three shots were fired immediately in front of us on our arrival. The unexpected explosions shook us, and their significance entered our consciousness. "Don't be afraid," said one of our escorts mockingly, "*those* shots were not for you" Those shots!

As we were led through the door into a room the attitude of politeness immediately changed. I was thrown down onto a mattress on the floor, Pearl onto another. We were warned not to say a word. With a slight manipulation I managed to see dimly through the cloth over my eyes.

On the floor in the corner of the room sat a man, blindfolded and handcuffed. He was being questioned, and from his answers I recognised the voice of Baruch, a man in the closest circle of my friends and in military service.

In another room there was the sound of rough movement and many angry voices. A girl was being goaded to hysterical anger and tears. It was the voice of another friend of mine—a girl born in Palestine, daughter of an Orthodox Jerusalem family.

Heavy-booted footsteps came across the floor of our room. A loud order was given to Baruch to stand up, and he was roughly pushed into the next room. Sounds of beating and slapping, voices screaming, more beating—then he was pushed back into our room and fell onto the floor panting.

Pearl and I were silent. A few minutes later she was led to the tribunal. An altercation of high voices followed. Then came my turn!

I was seated at a table opposite the polite civilian-clothed man who had called at the flat. There were many other figures surrounding me in the room. The handkerchief was removed from my eyes. The friendly face of my accuser had changed to an inhuman mask, the half closing of one eye adding to the sinister expression.

"You told me a pack of lies," he shouted at me. Before I had time to answer, he continued in the same loud, insulting, threatening voice: "You are a spy, a traitor from England. All your friends are your tools."

I tried to speak—it was useless. As I opened my mouth he turned on me again. "Do you know who we are?" he asked, and then added: "We are the Stern Gang; no doubt you have heard of us. We don't play—we act! We have an account to settle with Mr. Bevin—and with you. If you tell us the names of the people you are working for in England, we may spare your life. Otherwise, you will never leave here."

The absurdity of his accusations left me calm and silent. His temper increased and he raged at me. "It is no use you sitting there with that innocent face. It can't deceive me. It is a mask behind which you hide a whole network of espionage. Your only hope is to tell us the truth."

"I have told you the truth," I replied, "and I am very sorry I can't change my face." In his exasperation he was speechless, and he waved to a man to take me away. The handkerchief was again tied over my eyes. As I left he said: "In twenty-four hours' time you will speak differently."

I remember that the worst crimes were committed by the L.H.Y.—the Stern Gang! I noticed a cubicle next to our prison room. A woman was lying on the floor, covered with a blanket. She moaned as I passed. It was Mrs. H. My heart ached for my friends.

There were many footsteps in and out of the room, occasional shots outside the window, voices, noises. Someone else was brought in and taken to the other room. A loud accusing voice, an attempt to reply—hard thrashing. Another man was thrown on the floor of our room. Another friend! He was breathing painfully; I knew his heart was not strong as a result of concentration camps in Europe.

The four of us were strengthened by one another's presence and our guiltlessness. We were watched and threatened, and we obeyed the order to keep silent.

Some hours later the girl who was questioned first was sent home with a warning to end all association with me. The papers in the pocket of our friend who was brought in last showed unquestionable proof of his identity and activities. He, too, was released. There was no reprieve for me, nor for my friends Pearl and Baruch. Mrs. H. also was kept in the next cubicle.

The men in the other room left the house and a few soldiers remained to keep guard over us. We were under sentence of death and we were to be "induced" to admit our guilt and to disclose the names of all the spies and plans of espionage. I was supposed to be the ringleader.

We were given food—large chunks of bread, plates amply filled with noodles, sardines, and vegetables. It was a very hot afternoon; the cloth 'round my head and eyes made my head ache—I couldn't eat. I had no fears. God had protected me through so many dangers. He would not desert me now.

I asked for a drink of water. I was given a glass of paraffin! One of the young men on guard laughed with satisfaction as I unsuspectingly swallowed a mouthful. A little later a boy brought water and kneeled beside me, saying a prayer of blessing as he gave it to me. Another who had just arrived was full of sympathy. He whispered to me: "Have you no friends outside who could help you? Tell me their names."

I had many friends who might help, but I did not want to involve anyone else in this unhappy affair.

"I have one friend who will help me," I replied.

"Who?" he asked eagerly.

"God," I answered.

There was a constant clicking of guns and revolvers. Fingers played about with the guns as though itching to use them. Insults were hurled at Pearl and me. "Traitor!" "Spy!" "What did you come from England for?" "Two weeks ago we shot a woman like you outside here. We will shoot you all!"

Hard steel was prodded into my side. Rifle-ends were put up against my face. "Do you know what these are? You will know better still tomorrow morning."

Toward evening we were left with one young guard. He was kind and sympathetic. For a few moments he left us alone. Pearl was losing hope. "My poor daughter!" she cried softly, and gave me addresses and commissions to do for her after her death. "You will be freed," she said to me. "God protects you, but I have no hope."

Baruch's faith also wavered. "I am in uniform," he said. "They will finish me."

"Nonsense," I replied. "God will save us from this, but we must have no doubts. Let us pray together."

Our guard returned and heard us. "Be quiet," he ordered. We prayed on silently.

"Why did you do it?" he asked me. "Why did you betray our people?"

"Why don't you first make sure that I did betray our people instead of using these methods on innocent victims?" I answered.

"We must be severe and punish and kill all Jews who are not good Jews," he replied.

"It seems that we both want the same thing—that all Jews should be good Jews!"

There were many footsteps outside and our evening meal was brought in. "Eat your last meal," cried voices laughing, cruel, mocking. "Tomorrow morning at dawn …"

Another soldier sat on the guard's chair at the entrance of the room. I lifted the corner of the cloth over my eyes. "Put it down," he shouted at me. I tried to say something. "Shut your mouth," he cried.

But in that moment of looking I had seen enough. A devil sat on that chair; a devil in the form of a young man. I shuddered and prayed.

The evening shadows were falling. The sun had departed. A cold wind chased away all the lingering warmth. Barred windows and doors were open. I lay on the dirty mattress, wearing only thin summer clothes. Pearl had a blanket and asked for one for me. "No," came the reply, "she can't have a blanket."

The shadows deepened. The wind blowing through all the open doors and windows was chilled. I lay shivering with cold and with the consciousness of a devil on guard! All the voices outside died away in the distance. The horror of the night began.

After a few hours of torture through which Pearl, Baruch, and I were united by all the bonds of shared unspeakable suffering, endurance, and faith, at a moment when I almost cried, "O my God, why has Thou forsaken me?" footsteps came up the steps to the door and called the torturer away!

The door was closed and bolted. The devil was removed and locked out. For a short time we were alone. Oh, the blessed relief, the rescue from heaven! We were silent—not by order, but because we were beyond words.

Someone was trying to open the door! My heart stood still. Was the devil returning? The door would not open. A man was banging, pushing, hammering. Who had closed it so securely that it had to be broken open? At last it gave way. A man entered. A torch-light was flashed on me. "No blanket?" said a kind voice. "It is so cold. I shall try to find one for you."

An angel had come in! He also brought a blanket for Baruch. Under the cover of the blanket, spread over me by a kind hand, my bruised body relaxed and was warmed. Another guard sat on the chair at the door, a friendly reassuring voice—a boy's voice—the one who only wanted Jews to be good Jews.

The first pale rays of dawn came mysteriously through the barred windows. I was conscious of the silent fears of Pearl and Baruch. Was this to be the last time we would see the rays of dawn on this earth? What did this day hold in store for us?

I for my part wondered a little, but I knew I could leave it all to God. All the devils and all the guns in the world could not harm me if God had other plans for me—if there still was work for me to do.

All doubts left me—I still had work to do. I would see the dawn break over Israel many times yet. I would see the dark corners swept clean—the devils flee before the angels.

There were voices and footsteps approaching. The first mysterious light of dawn was changing. Shapes and lines were becoming more clearly defined. I looked at Pearl—a little figure crouching against the wall. In the other corner sat Baruch, his head resting on his knees.

Someone came in and roughly tightened the handkerchief over my eyes so that I could not see out of any corner. Suddenly the room was filled with people. Heavy boots moved around us. Many voices—of men and women. Much clicking of guns. A shot was fired from the door. They laughed, talked, insulted, mocked—sang death songs.

Our calmness exasperated them. The muzzle of a gun was pressed against my face; an ugly voice shouted in my ear—I did not understand the words. I felt boots and guns against my body.

The lack of the desired effect upon us caused the frustrated emotions to turn upon themselves, and before long the young men and women, who had come to goad us into fear and submission, were involved in a quarrel amongst themselves. After much noise and scuffling they disappeared and we were left alone with two guards.

"What now?" I asked.

"You must wait for our chief to come."

The dawn had passed; we were still alive! The hours of waiting were long. Before midday the "chief" and his retinue arrived. I was called to the other room.

The handkerchief was removed from my eyes. I sat opposite the man who had accused me the day before. "You are free!" he said, looking slightly embarrassed. The cruel expression of the previous day had changed and he was normal and calm again. I could see in his face the man had suffered, who had thought much, and who was seeking to serve Israel.

"I understand your motive for arresting me," I said. "It was your duty to investigate if you had any suspicion. I appreciate your efforts to rid Israel of all traitors, and am aware of the cases in which you have really unmasked those who betrayed their own people. But you make a great mistake by using such devilish methods in the treatment of your prisoners. You go one step too far and, instead of upholding the honour of our people, you bring further shame upon it."

He looked at me then put out a friendly hand as I rose to leave the room. For a moment I hesitated. Then I gave him my hand.

A few minutes later Pearl and Baruch heard the same words. We were free. Together we thanked God that he had prevented such a grave crime from taking place. An attempt had been made to destroy, not only our lives, but the honour of the whole Jewish people. It was in this dark corner of Israel that other deeds of terrorism had been conceived and committed, giving the world an opportunity to feed the germ of anti-Semitism.

Released from prison, I learned how friends had been told of my plight and had immediately contacted all authorities, until my identity had been established and sent with a warning to the "chief" of the Stern Gang who had kidnapped us. God moves in many ways to rescue those who believe in him.

The bruises and the bleeding scratches on my body soon healed. The memory of other horrors faded. There remained only the consciousness of the spiritual experiences of those twenty-four hours in the hands of the Stern Gang; the rays of light in the darkness.

CHAPTER NINE

DAWN

AUGUST, 1948–MAY, 1949

A few weeks after the second "cease fire" I received a telegram from my sister. She had arrived from South Africa and was in Tel Aviv. Permits were being given in special cases to leave Jerusalem. After much difficulty I succeeded in getting a permit to go to Tel Aviv to meet my sister. I booked a seat in a taxi.

BURMA ROAD

I was again on the Jerusalem road. It was almost seven months since my arrival in convoy, in an armoured car. This time I travelled in an open car—safe from the enemy! The first part of the journey was on the main road, passing the conquered Arab villages from which the dangerous attacks had come when I last travelled that way.

After forty minutes driving we left the main road, and attention and interest were increased. 'Round the rocky mountains and through the sandy plains a new road had been opened—the "Burma Road."

We were badly shaken as we passed over stony ways, not yet tarred and smoothed. We were covered with layers of dust as we laboured along sandy tracks. We walked uncomplainingly in the heat up a very steep hill, too difficult for the car to climb with its load of passengers. We relaxed with thankfulness as we sped over concreted, finished parts of the road. And all along the way we were acutely conscious of the uncovered pipe-line at the side of the road. We could "see" and "feel" the water that was flowing through it.

We were all very silent on the journey—silent with our thoughts. This road and this pipe-line had saved Jerusalem; saved its people from hunger and thirst. Built with the blood of soldiers and the sweat of the workers, it was the "miracle" behind the victory of the battle for Jerusalem.

We passed ghost-like deserted Arab villages—empty, half-destroyed clay huts and stone houses. We arrived in Tel Aviv exhausted, uncomfortably hot and dusty, but with a deep sense of victory and thankfulness. There I met my sister again! There was much to be told of the experiences of the three years since we had parted in Jerusalem.

Tel Aviv had come to life again. The streets were filled with people, mainly in uniform; the shops were doing business. The first thing I did when I reached the hotel was to turn on the tap in the bathroom. The water flowed. "Use as much as you want," I was told. "There is no shortage of water here."

MALAYA ROAD

A few weeks later I returned to Jerusalem. It was a much easier and quicker journey. Parts of the "Burma Road" were no longer used; there was another road—the "Malaya Road"! There were long stretches of finished road and many workers putting all their energy into getting the other parts completed before the rains set in. All man-power from Jerusalem was used, everyone giving a certain period of time for work on the road. The water-pipe was being covered and protected.

On December 7th the road was officially opened. It was the most vital and decisive factor in the victory of the war for Jerusalem. The blood of heroes sprinkled the sands and washed the stones.

Another miracle was added to the long list of miracles in the history of the people of Israel that had saved them from their enemies.

The nicknames "Burma Road" and "Malaya Road" were dropped. The new life-line to Jerusalem now bears its own well-earned name—"*Kvish Hagevura*" (Courage Road). The road of courage, strength, and faith!

BONDS: FEBRUARY 1949

Now the war is over. The armistice with Egypt has been signed. Peace negotiations are taking place with the other Arab States. Britain has finally recognised the State of Israel and has been followed by a number of other States.

The streets of Jerusalem are filled with strangers. One hears many languages—from visitors curious to see Jerusalem after the siege. Many who left the city a year ago are returning. Business improves and the life of the world flows in again.

But beneath this stream of new life there is a life that cannot be touched by any outside hand. There is a bond uniting the people of Jerusalem who shared the days of the siege, which deepens as the clouds lift, letting in a new light on the city.

I went to buy my rations. The shop was filled with people, old customers and new. I remembered the days when I was the only one who called for rations—sometimes only a couple of slices of bread, or a few pieces of *matzoth*—when my neighbours could not leave their children alone in the shelters for the shells were bursting all around.

The shopkeeper gave me my rations and besides these he offered me a large selection of many desirable foodstuffs. He showed a special warmth as he served me. There was a silent understanding. He, too, remembered.

I looked in at the window of the florist's shop at the corner I had passed daily during the siege. For months it had been closed—at that time there were no flowers in Jerusalem. I saw some in pots in which the first green leaves of tulip bulbs were piercing the earth. I entered and asked if I could buy one.

"Not yet," said the young man in the shop apologetically. "These are my last bulbs, and it is hard to part with them. My whole garden, glasshouses, and plants were completely destroyed during the fight. We cannot import any more bulbs from Holland. Israel needs more important things. I want to watch these grow for a while before I sell them. They mean more to me than money."

Then he looked at me again. I had bought a few flowers every Friday until he closed his shop and went to the battle. He remembered and began to talk to me of the dangerous job he had done—still a secret. Of how, on one occasion, twenty-five of his comrades lay dead around him. How he had brought his ration of food home to feed his children whenever it had been possible to go home. He recalled again the many miracles he had experienced during the fight for Jerusalem.

"I thank God that I have been saved and brought back to my family," he said. "My brother was seriously wounded and will be an invalid for the rest of his life."

We looked again at the tulip bulbs bursting with the promise of their hidden beauty. We both remembered.

THE NEW STATE: MARCH 1949

It is now nearly a year since the birth of the State of Israel. Throughout the whole period war has continued, but with abated fury. During the latter months Jerusalem had been comparatively quiet. Hostilities flared up in other parts of Israel. In the Negev the Egyptians were defeated.

Notwithstanding the strain of war, the drain on resources of man-power and money, the interruption of all economic life, the young State has grown and developed. The life of Israel is vigorous, and the young State matures rapidly. Israel has embraced its people with a new responsibility. The provisional government has been preparing the way for the elected government of the people. The first census was taken in November.

Jerusalem is being cleaned up; damaged buildings are being repaired; road blocks and the untidiness of barbed wire, sandbags, and other objects of defence are cleared away. Shops that had been partly destroyed or closed are being put in order and reopened. The bomb-damaged Jewish Agency building has been restored. Shell holes in the streets are being filled in.

With the clearing away of the ravages of war in the streets there has also been a spiritual cleaning up. After the murder of Count Bernadotte by Jews the government of Israel was determined to root out this destructive growth from the soil it was polluting. There was a thorough hunt for the murderers; all movement throughout the country was checked. All the members of the Stern Gang were arrested.

The dark places in Israel are being swept clean. The prison house where my friends and I had been tortured—where women had been shot without trial—is no longer a prison house.

ELECTIONS

It was the eve of the elections. The streets of Jerusalem were festively decorated. Prized had been offered for the best-dressed window. Every little shop had made an effort. There were gatherings and speeches and loud-speakers in many streets. The Jewish flag was flying from all windows.

I remembered a day in Berlin when Hitler was broadcasting to the German people. From the heavily charged air in the silenced streets came the voice, the loud hysterical voice, the voice that opposed the power of world destiny and clamoured for the destruction of the Jewish race and the staining of the earth with Jewish blood.

Now the blue and white flag of Israel, with the Star of David, is flying from the windows of its own home—in the city of its own land—Jerusalem!

The day of the elections passed in solemn quietness. All the shops were closed. The Jewish people were voting in their own country, choosing their own government. They were free to lead their lives according to their own laws and principles, free to build a new life—free to be Jews!

Some weeks later I walked again through the streets of Jerusalem. From the Eden Hotel, along the King George Avenue to the Jewish Agency, the streets were lined with dense crowds. Military police kept the way clear. The people were silent and waited patiently. It was an important occasion. Even the clouds in the sky seemed to pass over Jerusalem with greater solemnity.

The advance guard of white-helmeted, uniformed motorcyclists started their engines, followed by a procession of slowly moving cars, conveying the representatives of different States of the world to the Jewish Agency building.

All eyes were fixed on the door of the Eden Hotel. At last the silence was broken. Cheering broke out in the crowds. Chaim Weizmann, the man who had worked for Zionism and had been such a vital part of its life for so many years, stood for a few moments before entering the waiting car. Beside him was his wife, his companion through the many long years of struggle. They warmly acknowledged the greeting of the people. Then the frail man, spent in years and health, proceeded on his way to the Agency building to be made President, the first President of the State of Israel!

The heart of Jerusalem beat painfully when the State was born. The heart of Jerusalem beats happily as it feels the first steps of the new life being taken on its soil.

EIN KAREM

Immigrants were arriving in great numbers at the ports of Haifa and Tel Aviv and were being dispersed into all parts of Israel. The abandoned Arab houses in the suburbs of Jerusalem were being filled with people from all the countries of the world. Organisations were being formed to deal with all the needs and problems of this inflowing stream of people—the surviving remnants of persecution who had suffered much and waited long for freedom to enter their own land.

The long winter was coming to an end, and on the first day when the sun shone with warmth from a cloudless blue sky I went to Ein Karem. My last visit there had been three years ago in 1946. I remembered the primitive Arab homes, the Arab women gathered 'round the pool in the centre of the village doing their washing, the men sitting in the open café smoking their *nargilehs*.

On one hillside was the ornate modern Russian church. Houses belonging to the church were scattered in the gardens reaching to the top of the hill. Across the olive-clad valley, on the opposite hill, was another church.

There had been hard fighting around Ein Karem before the Arabs fled. It was out of bounds for a long time. Now, on the first day of spring of 1949, it was good to be able to pay another visit to that lovely village, nestling between and on the hills—the birthplace of John the Baptist.

A new life was thrusting its roots into the soil; a life born of this land which, after being transplanted into all the other lands of this world, was now returning to be replanted into its mother soil.

I wandered through little lanes and cobbled alleys between primitive houses. Hidden in the peaceful sunny loveliness, which shone through the flower-decked trees and scented the earth's breath, there was a mysterious activity. The land of Israel was welcoming its children back with a love that was breaking down the strangeness, the hesitating shyness and restraint of a family long separated from its home.

A young man looked out of a door with a friendly smile.

"How long have you been here?" I asked.

"Two weeks," he replied. "From Hungary. Come up and see our room."

I walked up a few very precarious steps made of stone.

"Quite safe now," the man called out. "Only half of them were there when we came."

Inside a young woman was cleaning and arranging a few belongings. The man proudly showed us the wardrobe he had made from pieces of wood left behind by the Arabs.

It was a large room and the young couple were energetically and happily making it their home. "They gave us this room a few days after we arrived," he said. "I am a tailor and shall start working here immediately. Ein Karem is a beautiful place."

Life, hope, happiness shone from the faces of the young man and his wife. He pointed to a small stony square opposite his room. "That will be my garden!" he said, "and there I shall keep my chickens." One could see through his eyes—the stones transformed!

Further along the lane, in a little courtyard, a woman invited me with a smile to see her room. A very large room with four beds, and in the corner a stove, upon which a big saucepan of food was cooking. "My husband works in Jerusalem," she said. "He is a tinsmith. My children also go there to school. They come home every evening. We have been here a month—from Morocco."

She showed me another room and a kitchen, which were not yet ready for use. Then she sat on her chair near the stove.

"You have a very nice place," I said. "Aren't you happy?"

"Yes, it is good," she replied, then shrugged her shoulders without another word. The transplanted life had not yet taken root firmly.

I wandered along and looked through many doors into rooms, large and small, still unoccupied, but clean whitewashed and ready to receive their new occupants. From other rooms I heard the sound of hammer and saw: much activity in the making of homes—homes for the people who had been homeless for so long, driven from one place to another—persecuted, tortured. They were making homes—homes in their own land. Free to work, to build, to create—to live!

In one little street there was a box attached to a wooden post and in the open box a shelf on which a pair of shoes was displayed—the first showcase! Opposite lived the shoemaker. There were many customers already 'round him. He had come from Bulgaria a few weeks before. "It is good to be here," he said, his face shining. "It is good to be in Ein Karem."

A man passed by with a dark face and an angry voice. "I am leaving this place at once," he yelled. "It is not fit for anyone to live in. How can they expect us to live here? I will not remain another day."

"When did you come?" I asked.

"Yesterday!"

While he was talking another man came along, carrying a heavy load on his shoulder and singing. He glared at the one who had complained, then shouted after him heatedly:

"The sooner you get out of here the better," adding a word in Chinese that I did not understand. He turned to me.

"We both came from China, on the same ship. We fled there from Hitler. Such a man should be drowned, not brought to Israel! How many good Jews were killed in gas chambers and such a skunk is allowed to live, and to be brought to Israel!"

He shook with anger and shouted another unintelligible word in the direction of the offender. "I am a butcher," he said. "I arrived yesterday and shall open my shop tomorrow." He continued on his way with a firm step, carrying his load on his back and singing songs of Israel.

I passed rooms filled with new arrivals waiting to be sorted out and placed. The little café had started business. Two men were unpacking their goods, one from Russia, the other from Czechoslovakia. The only drink obtainable that day was *Lebben* (sour milk), which I drank with thankfulness. "Tomorrow we shall have tea and coffee," I was told.

The blue in the sky was deepening. The blossoms on the trees were more intensely white and pink. Curls of pale smoke were rising from home fires. Spring was in the air, in the earth, and in the people. A new life was unfolding.

INDEPENDENCE DAY

May 4, 1949! A year (according to the Jewish calendar) since the British Mandatory Power left Palestine and Israel declared its political independence! The first anniversary of the birth of a free State of Israel! A year of sacrifice, pain, and hardship—a year of achievement, victory, and freedom.

Flags are flying from every window—the blue and white flag with the Star of David. Preparations for this celebration have been going on for days, and on the eve of this day of remembrance and rejoicing the crowds have gathered in the central streets of the city.

The voice of the Prime Minister came through the loudspeakers in Zion Square, proclaiming the festival of freedom as the third in Jewish history; the first the exodus from Egypt over three thousand years ago; the second the victory of Judah the Maccabee over the Syro-Greek defilers of the Temple, more than two thousand years ago.

Then he said: "Our security cannot depend on strength alone; it must rest also on justice and progress at home."

As the evening darkened into night, the crowds in and around Zion Square became more dense. Groups of young people joined hands and danced the *Hora*, a Jewish national dance. Music, singing, and laughter filled the square, which a year ago was so empty and desolate under the bombardment of shells, mortar bombs, and bullets.

In the empty space in Ben Yehuda Street, surrounded by the tidied ruins of shattered buildings, on a wall next to what was once the Atlantic Hotel, where so many had been killed by explosives left in a lorry at the side of the road—a film was being shown: pictures of free Israel.

It is the morning of "Independence Day." The sun shines brightly upon Jerusalem. The synagogues are filled with thankful worshippers. In the streets the crowds are gathering, lining the route along which the military parade will pass.

In King George Avenue a reviewing stand has been erected. Roofs, balconies, and windows in the vicinity are filled with men, women, and children waiting expectantly for the display of military strength, which has been arranged to celebrate this day of festival.

I have a seat on the balcony of Pearl's flat, overlooking the reviewing stand and the waiting masses of people. From this same balcony I have watched so many other scenes during the past year: the wounded picked up in the street after shell explosions;

the damaged armoured cars being towed in after the battles; the lorries with their piled wooden boxes, containing the remains of heroes; the funeral processions; the first convoy with food during the siege.

There was a momentary silence in the crowds as three mounted cavalrymen led the parade past the reviewing stand. Cheering broke out from the crowds as a number of mounted flag-bearers followed. The flag of Israel waved triumphantly through the streets of Jerusalem.

Then came the march past of the different brigades. The young men, the young women, the old veterans—those who had been trained in the British army, those I had seen in groups in the streets a year ago, receiving their first instructions. They all marched by with full military consciousness—an army in their own land, formed to defend their land; an army that had faced the enemy victoriously!

I watched the parade with mixed feelings. As a pacifist I had always turned away from military parades and displays of military strength. But as I watched this army march past—the men, the women, the small number of armoured cars, lorries, and other equipment—I saw them again as I had seen them during the past year. I saw those who passed in the parade—and those who cheered them on the way. There was no difference. They were one—the people of Israel, who had defended their homeland.

I saw the men and women who had not known how to hold a gun, who knew nothing of military tactics; who went out in small groups to face great numbers of the enemy; who, with hardly any equipment or training, won victory after victory. I knew that this army had saved us from the horrors that would have befallen us had we been delivered into the hands of the Arabs and our other enemies.

I felt a deep thankfulness for all the miracles that showed the hand of God at work amongst his people Israel; but in my heart was the prayer that I may soon see the day when the further promise of God will be fulfilled. The day when "they shall beat their swords into plowshares, and their spears into pruning hooks;

nation shall not lift up their sword against nation, neither shall they learn war any more."

Another chapter has come to an end in the history of the Jewish people; another page has been turned in the Book of Destiny. The Jewish people have their State. God has saved them again from destruction. And now, "O house of Jacob, come ye and let us walk in the way of the LORD."

PSALM 126

When the LORD turned again the captivity of Zion,
    we were like them that dream.
Then was our mouth filled with laughter,
    and our tongue with singing;
then they said among the heathen,
    "The LORD hath done great things for them."
The LORD hath done great things for us;
    whereof we are glad.
Turn again our captivity, O LORD,
    as the streams in the south!
They who sow in tears
    shall reap in joy!
He that goeth forth and weepeth,
    bearing precious seed,
shall doubtless come again with rejoicing,
    bringing his sheaves with him.

PART III

UNLESS THE LORD BUILDS THE HOUSE

CHAPTER TEN

THE BIRTH OF THE STATE OF ISRAEL

O n September 4 (1949) the Jerusalem Fellowship and the Messianic Jewish Community held a conference at the Conway Hall, London. It was attended by friends in and around London and there were also friends from the north and west country. The spirit of love and fellowship that pervaded the meeting, uniting Jew and Gentile sharing a common vision, was an inspiring promise of the greater unity of mankind, which is to come with the establishment of God's rule on earth. Besides giving new zeal and encouragement to those present it served also as a reminder of the responsibility laid upon all to whom the vision of the coming kingdom is revealed.

The momentous events of the past year and the manifold experiences through which God had brought the Community in Jerusalem provided the background to the messages of the different speakers, giving them a sense of reality and of the urgency of the times. The protection and guidance of God experienced by the Community in Jerusalem was a source of encouragement to all the friends gathered. They could thus share in the gratitude to God of those more immediately concerned with the work and rejoice with them at his doing in the midst of Israel.

EXPERIENCES IN JERUSALEM

Pauline Rose, who returned from Jerusalem a week before the conference, spoke about her personal experiences in the Holy City during the siege, when the Jewish section of the city was surrounded by the enemy, cut off from all means of supply, help, or communication; of the heroic stand of the people, who won victory after victory in the face of overwhelming odds; of the spirit that guided them during that period, showing clearly the hand of God working to bring out the fulfilment of his plan.

"The birth of the State of Israel," she said, "was a milestone in the destiny of the Jewish people, a most important event in the history of mankind. The victories of the war were won in the power of God, but now the State develops on human lines, with all the weaknesses and shadows of the human government. With the establishment of the State of Israel we stand on the bridge that leads to the Kingdom of Israel, and only with the return of the King of Israel will the bridge be crossed and the people governed by the full power of the Spirit.

"The mission of the Messianic Jewish Community, during the time of war, was to remain united in Jerusalem—in the midst of the people, to pray for peace, and to keep the light of the Messiah burning in Israel. Most Gentile and Jewish Christians had left the country at the beginning of the danger period. It was the task of the small group of Jews that had formed our Community to be the witness for the Messiah in all the circumstances of war during those dark days in Jerusalem.

"During the whole war period a room was preserved for us in the centre of the bomb-damaged city, where the Sabbath service was never missed, and where we had our daily meetings for prayer and fellowship. Through all the dangers of bullets and shells, as well as other trials of war, this was a haven of peace for our community. The power of the spirit that protected it was also felt by strangers around us who were drawn to us in time of danger and found peace in our midst.

"Now we have a small home with an upper room facing the Mount of Olives—a room practically destroyed during the battle, but now restored as a sanctuary of prayer. Through its window we look out upon the place where Yeshua ascended from the earth, and there we pray daily for his return.

"The Community is very small, we are still very weak and imperfect instruments, but we believe that we are being tested and formed for a future task. We do not try to "gather in" numbers: it is our principle to remain small and in the background, waiting for God to send his chosen ones, and to guide us step by step. Many interested inquirers have come to us from all circles of Jewish life.

"In Jerusalem the Satanic attacks against all Christian witnesses are very severe, and the Messianic Jewish Community is a prize target for these attacks. We have few friends in Israel. Neither Jews nor Gentiles understand us or approve of us. Therefore, we need the support of our friends in all countries outside of Israel. Your prayers build a protective spiritual wall around us, and your material help contributes to the needs of the daily life in this work of God. There are many who come to us in great need of spiritual and material help. Our door is always open.

"At present we stand on the 'bridge,' our numbers are small, our way not yet fully opened. We are being prepared, dependent entirely upon God's guidance. We expect great events in the future. It may be years before our time comes for public activity and greater numbers, but it may even be tomorrow. We do not know. Only God knows in which way he wishes to use us. He chooses his instruments. He appoints his time. We must endure the period of preparation and purification, we must have patience to wait, and be ready at any moment for orders to change our plans.

"With the birth of the State of Israel we know that the Kingdom of Israel is not far off. With that vision before us we are strengthened to bear the trials that precede the time of God's kingdom on earth, and are ready to leave everything and follow the call of the Messiah."

CHAPTER ELEVEN
THE POWER OF THE SPIRIT

The fact that I am in Germany today and present at this conference,[16] is of the deepest significance for me personally, and shows me more clearly than ever before the mighty power of the Spirit and the wonder of God's grace. My last visit to Germany was in 1936, when I came to look for my relatives who were among the first of Hitler's victims. Some I found in hiding, others disappeared without leaving a trace behind. At that time I was still far from the knowledge of Messiah. I was filled with horror, fear, and shame, and a helplessness that led to despair. I left Germany vowing within myself that I would never again set foot in the country, nor have contact with anything or anyone connected with it. But God had other intentions for me.

I hated Christianity because of the crimes perpetrated by a so-called Christian nation. I was in some way ashamed of my people for being in a position to be so cruelly and criminally treated. I looked for God and could not find him. I felt completely lost. Then, in my despair, Yeshua revealed himself to me. From one moment to the next I was transported from the depths of despair to the heights of joy. From that time the Spirit began the work of transformation within me and I saw Yeshua not only as my personal Saviour, but also as the Messiah of Israel.

With this revelation hidden mysteries were unveiled and I could see all events taking their places marked on God's plan of

---

[16] Stuttgart Conference, 1953.

salvation. Horror gave place to understanding, fear changed to faith, and shame to repentance and rejoicing. I speak of this personal experience because it is the manifestation of the working of the Spirit in the individual, the miracle that will eventually take place in every individual when the kingdom of God is established on earth and Messiah rules in every heart.

THE MESSIANIC JEWISH COMMUNITY

The next factor that led to my return to Germany was the coming into being of the Messianic Jewish Community. With the regathering of the Jewish people and the restoration of their State there was also the beginning of their conversion— the Messianic Jewish Community. My mission was shown to me—to serve with this Community.

I would have rejoiced to see my people at home again in their land even if I had not known the Messiah, but I could never have come to Germany. Only he could bring me back. Today I realise more fully the meaning of God's grace; without it I could not have been present at this conference—hate would still have been in my heart.

It is only with the spirit of Messiah in our hearts and the vision of his kingdom before us that we can understand the meaning of a restored Israel and the mission of the Messianic Jewish Community. With this understanding we can also see the working of the Spirit bringing it to pass. While I was in Jerusalem during the siege and birth of the State of Israel, I witnessed and experienced daily the miracles wrought by God for the victory of his people and confusion of the enemy.

CALL TO GERMAN CHRISTIANS

Now, today, I see another manifestation of Messiah's victory. Here in Germany, where Satan used all his powers in an effort to destroy the Jews, Messiah now calls out a people to support and help the Jews. Here, where on my last visit I experienced nothing but hatred toward me and my people, now I experience the love of friends who are united with us in this mission of preparation for the approaching kingdom of Israel's Messiah—a mission of prayer and repentance.

It is difficult to express how deeply moved I am by this experience of God's grace and love, and the uniting power of Messiah's spirit, which lifts us from the darkness of hate and separation to the light of love and unity, making us one— Jew and Gentile, Jew and German. How else could this unity be achieved?

MESSIANIC JEWS AND GENTILES

In London there is a community of Jews and Gentiles, who over a number of years, through many tests and trials, have become deeply united in love and service and are a powerful witness for the "oneness" of Jew and Gentile in Messiah. The members of this Community come from different denominations and religious circles, some remaining members of their church or group, others having become separated from the circles to which they belonged previously. Each one is free to follow his own convictions; but in spirit, vision, and service our Gentile brethren are one with the Messianic Jewish Community, bound by the Messiah in an inseparable bond.

This Community in London is also a strong spiritual centre of prayer supporting the work in Germany and united with all the prayer circles that have come into being in this country. From this centre in London contacts are made with many of the other English speaking countries. Recently we have seen the Spirit at work in other lands calling out brethren who share our vision, strengthening the ranks of the Brotherhood and deepening the unity in prayer. From Australia, New Zealand, South Africa, Jamaica, India come letters assuring us of their loving support in prayer, their unity in spirit.

SIGNS OF THE KINGDOM

We are living in times when the powers of light and darkness are becoming manifest in an ever increasing measure. We see many miracles happening before our eyes every day; but let us not dwell too long upon the miracles themselves but upon the One who has the power to perform these miracles. He has brought us through all the pitfalls that were set for us in the darkness, and if we keep our eyes fixed upon him we will be carried over all the traps set for us now and in the future. We have seen the manifestation of the Spirit within ourselves, in Israel, in Germany and also in other countries; these are but the first beginnings of the realisation of God's great plan of salvation for mankind.

While we are being filled with the joy of the wonders we are now experiencing, let us look toward those still greater wonders being prepared for us by our Father in heaven—the wonders of his kingdom.

This great joy and thankfulness which we experience today in this Brotherhood of the Messiah, will one day be experienced by all peoples. It is a token of life in the kingdom under the rule of Messiah on earth. With this vision clearly before us let us not be distracted by any shadow that may fall on our path, but keep our gaze fixed upon our Leader, who guides us toward his kingdom in Israel, and wants us to pray for Jerusalem, the city of his throne and for his witnesses in Israel who carry his banner in the midst of his people:

> Let all those who put their trust in Thee rejoice: let them ever shout for joy because Thou defendest them: let them also that love Thy name be joyful in Thee.

CHAPTER TWELVE
THE CHOSEN (AN ALLEGORY)

M any are called, but few are chosen." Who is called? There was once an officer, a faithful and devoted servant of his king. One day he received an order from the king to take a little box with a great treasure inside to a distant land, and to deliver it there on a specific date.

Proud and honoured that this task had been given over to him, the officer was conscious of the importance of his mission and was completely sure that nothing could stop him from accomplishing the king's order.

For months he travelled through lands with great dangers; he overcame all obstacles and carefully preserved the precious box. Eventually he reached the last station of his journey. Only a river separated him from his goal, and he still had three days' time.

He was content with himself and resolved to rest during the night and to cross the river the next morning in a boat or over a bridge downstream. He looked for a place to rest for the night and found a little shack on the bank in which a poor fisherman offered him his bed, shared his simple meal with him, and provided for all his needs.

That night a severe thunderstorm began to rage over the entire land; downpours caused the river to overflow its banks. It appeared as if heaven had aimed for this particular river. The thunderstorm continued day and night. The bridge was destroyed and swept away; little boats were ripped from their anchors and carried away by the water.

The officer was desperate. There was only one more day until the box had to be delivered. But there was no bridge and no boat and the current was too dangerous to ford. He fell asleep, but the howling of the wind and the sound of heavy rain awakened him again and again throughout the night. His heart sank. He could not deliver the box in the morning; he could not fulfil his mission.

The fisherman had great pity for the officer. He did not know how important his task was or how valuable the treasure in the box was. He saw only how much the man suffered because he could not deliver the little box to the house on the other bank, and he sincerely wished to help him.

While the officer still slept, the fisherman took the box next to the bed, tied it securely to his back, and prayed to his heavenly Father to bring him safely to the other side. Then he defied the storm and jumped into the dangerous water in order to swim across.

At daybreak, after several hours of perilous struggle with the elements, he finally reached the other side, bloody and nearly unconscious. The box, which he had so securely tethered, still lay safely on his back. With utmost exhaustion he pulled himself up the riverbank until, at his last breath, he fell at the gate of the house to which the package was to be delivered.

The task was completed—just in time. But who was the chosen one? The king's honoured officer, his friend? Or the poor fisherman, who humbly and unsuspectingly sought only to serve his neighbour?

The officer was a faithful, trustworthy servant who believed he could carry out the king's order. He also indeed travelled far and overcame many obstacles. He looked after the valuable treasure and brought it to the last station of the journey—but then he relaxed before he had fulfilled his obligation and was also not ready to venture his life in the dangerous waters of the storm-churned river.

The poor fisherman, who was not aware of any special task and who did not know what kind of treasure he carried, was however willing to stake his life for his neighbour. With faith in

God and with a heart full of love, he carried out a task of greatest importance for his king.

Many who are called can make it to the last station—up to the dangerous river. But only a few can jump into the water, because they are ready to stake their lives for their neighbour.

They are the chosen, who follow Messiah, who carry out the orders of their King, and who inherit the kingdom of God. In this world they receive no honour, but one day they will be honoured by their King, whom they follow, because they are the children of the kingdom—the chosen ones.

CHAPTER THIRTEEN

OUR KNOWLEDGE IS IMPERFECT

O ur yearning is to understand perfectly the Word of God, but, "before that which is perfect arrives, we only see by means of a mirror, dimly, for we only know in part."

We cannot search for the truth unless we lift up our hearts in prayer unceasingly, free of all influence, unwavering before prejudices and dogma, in complete submission to our God. Only the spirit of Messiah, the spirit of patience, can protect us and guide us through the dangers that accompany the search for knowledge. This spirit is like the rope that binds a group of mountain climbers—it unites them, it binds them to the guide, it guards them from falling, and it helps the weaker ones. But the enemy blocks their path with rocks and stones that to them seem insurmountable.

We still cannot comprehend the secrets of God. We cannot form an opinion for ourselves apart from the light that we have received. The theologians may dispute everything, and the scholars may always find a biblical citation that supports their point of view; however, "the truth was hidden from the sages and intellectuals, and has been revealed to children."

It is good to gather together to study the Scriptures, but we must always remember that "I could understand all mysteries and all knowledge … but if I have not love, I am nothing."

Our differences in opinion could themselves be a blessing to us if our discussions on the Scriptures are conducted in a spirit of love and trust, and if we understand that these questions and responses are exchanged according to the light that has been given us.

We therefore understand that only Messiah, the Rock, is a sure support for us; we are not in safety unless we are united in his love. For it is precisely when we *ask questions*, when we do not yet see everything "face to face," that Satan lies in wait for us. For the enemy it is an opportunity to spread discord, for we see through a mirror dimly and Satan takes advantage of it by projecting his own images. He can say, "It is written," just as he did when he tempted Yeshua in the desert. He can spread doubt, just as he did with Eve.

God gives understanding and knowledge to "children," to those who wait patiently in prayer and in love.

It is sufficient for us to know that by the blood of Messiah our sins are pardoned, that he is the Lord, and that he will return and establish his kingdom on earth.

When will this be? No one knows. It is less important still for us to know when and in what manner his kingdom will be established than it is for us to prepare the way for Him by following our King according to the example he has given us, by "doing the will of our Father who is in heaven and loving Him with all our heart and all our strength."

At the time he has designated, he will give us understanding and will reveal all secrets to us, and "we will know as we have never known before. Now only three things abide: faith, hope, and love; but the greatest of these is love" (1 Corinthians 13:13).

CHAPTER FOURTEEN
RETURN TO JERUSALEM

I returned to Jerusalem on 2 February 1953 after an absence of three and a half years. At our arrival that night to the airfield in Lydda,[17] an Israeli airline stewardess boarded our aeroplane to greet us with these words: "Welcome to Israel!" A few minutes later, I once again found myself in the Holy Land, in Israel.

Aeroplanes from many countries landed and took off. An intense traffic dominated the airfield. Over the tower of the terminal flew, most predominantly, the flag of Israel, the flag with the Star of David. The same symbol could be found on the Israeli aeroplanes.

I think back to my previous arrival in Lydda in January 1948. At that time everything was sombre, silent, and threatening. The clouds of war weighed heavily upon the country; each footstep held danger. We still knew nothing of the sufferings that were to precede the moment when the Israeli flag would be raised, nor of the miracles that would make it possible.

The road from Lydda to Jerusalem was then still controlled by the enemy. I now travel in a free country. I once made the journey in the darkness of an armoured vehicle, while today I enjoy the luxury of a taxi; through its windows I could perceive the silhouette of the Judaean mountains standing out in the clear night sky, in which the stars appear more brilliant than any other place in the world.

Just a little before midnight I arrived in Jerusalem.

---

[17] [Present day Ben Gurion Airport.]

A WORLD OF CONTRASTS

As soon as I found myself in the streets of the city the next morning, I was overcome with new impressions that completely contrasted the memories of my previous stay. So many things had changed. The population had doubled, with new immigrants coming mainly from Morocco, Iraq, Persia, Yemen, Bulgaria, and Romania. Actually, the population of Jerusalem includes more than 50 percent of easterners of dark complexion.

The inhabitants of Jerusalem, with whom I lived through the siege and the war, who fought, suffered, and sacrificed themselves to defend Jerusalem, have intermingled with the new population in an extraordinary manner.

Jerusalem has always been a world of contrasts and extremes, in the natural realms as well as in the spiritual. Today these contrasts are more visible still. Among the immigrants one finds men from North Africa or from the Middle East, in which the standard of life has not surpassed the primitive existence of their ancestors who lived thousands of years beforehand; side by side with them in the immigrant camps lived some men who came to know a better life in modern European countries. Here we must face hard reality and fight to begin to unify a people who have come from all parts of the world, carrying the customs and influences of all the countries that have lodged them during the past two thousand years.

Zion Square, the centre of the new city, at times has the appearance of an oriental bazaar; men and women crouching on the ground, selling nuts, melons, and sunflower seeds, as well as candies, while some of the children with their high-pitched cries compete to be the first to offer their merchandise to the passersby. An elderly blind couple, draped in metres of lavish but faded oriental cloth, traverse the crowd guided by a child. A woman passes by; she is wearing an elegant fur coat, bright red Turkish pants that are tight at the ankles, and on her head she has placed a filthy turban over her two long braids.

Some blind people, paralytics, and beggars covered with scars stretch out their hands requesting alms. A priest in black, a tourist in modern clothing, young and vigorous Israeli soldiers, sorrowful women with children in their arms—all of these are part of the daily crowd that passes through the streets of Jerusalem.

In this world, which was strange to me, I recognised some traces of the life that I had known here a few years ago. The man who had cleared a corner of his shop, which had been destroyed by explosive shells, in order to try to save something of his merchandise and offer the client his sparse commodities in such great demand, had rebuilt his store and courageously attempted to adapt his life to the present conditions. That old shoeshine is still in the same place, the one who, the day that an explosive shell made a hole in the ground right in his usual spot, simply placed a few boards over the hole after wiping up the blood in order to set up his business on top of it and wait on clientele; he must now fight against many struggles caused by the competition, for numerous are the new-comers to his trade.

Those, and even many others with whom I lived through Jerusalem's dark hours, greet me joyfully. A bond unites us, a certain mutual understanding that nothing could destroy. The defenders of Jerusalem who fight against the enemy must now fight to resolve the problems posed by the regathering of a people that has been dispersed throughout the centuries—the very goal of their fight for the establishment of the State of Israel.

Many buildings still carry some "battle wounds." Certain ones have been rebuilt, new shops and new houses have been erected, and large housing units are about to be completed.

Barbed wire still surrounds the "no man's land" where some abandoned houses have been occupied by the homeless, risking their lives. Piles of rubble still indicate the border that separates Jerusalem; Jerusalem, a city split in two, in which half is Israeli and the other is Trans-Jordanian.

An armistice put an end to the hostilities without, however, leading to peace. Enemy sentries pace back and forth on the rooftop of a house on the other side of the street, in Trans-Jordanian territory; our soldiers stand guard from this side of the street. Now and again a gunshot serves as a reminder of 1948, warning of that which could come again. Complete stiffening of East-West relations, as well as complete relaxation of the tension, have had instant repercussions in Jerusalem.

All the spiritual forces are represented in Jerusalem; in its population all the points of the globe are assembled. The spirit of unity that animated the city during the entire siege has given room to a much darker spirit. In this realm the contrasts are sharp: violence and love, deception and kindness, egotism and the spirit of sacrifice walk alongside each other and collide with one another unceasingly.

Just as the city, the population itself is diversified by various foreign influences, barriers in language and in behaviour, and by spiritual differences, which are greater still. Innumerable political parties fight for supremacy, and plenty of religious groups prevent the union of the Jewish people. These groups range from the free-thinking liberal Jew to the strictest Orthodox Jew, and from the Canaanites who reject the God of Israel to the Messianic Jew who recognises that Yeshua is the Messiah.

THE UPPER ROOM

Entirely engrossed in these thoughts and these such diverse impressions I arrived at the Street of the Prophets, the gathering place of the Messianic Jewish Community.

A narrow, spiral staircase led me to the "upper room" and I found myself once more in the sanctuary, the centre of prayer. Through the window I saw a picture that has always remained vivid in my memory—the Mount of Olives. Since 1948, this "upper room" has been the working centre of the Messianic Community in Israel. The Sabbath lights, lit here week after week, have greatly strengthened the bonds that unite all those whom God has called from amongst Israel, and they have eliminated every foreign spirit.

Access to this "upper room" has always been for me as the entrance into a new world—a harbour of peace, a sanctuary of light and love. I joyfully return to all those who have remained faithful since the beginning of the work in Israel, and I made the acquaintance of all those who have joined our ranks these past three years.

We have always prayed that the Community would be as a beacon in the darkness that hangs over Israel, and this darkness has become deeper still during these last few years. But on that day I was aware of the light—the light of the Messiah—that shines in the heart of the Messianic Community in Israel.

COMMUNITY OF LOVE

The members of our community live in Jerusalem, in conditions that are difficult to comprehend by those abroad. They live under the attentive and jealous watch of Satan—but also under the protection of the love of Messiah. We feel these two forces incessantly within us and all around us, and we are aware of their constant battling. The satanic army is always ready to intervene at the slightest human failure; but the army of the Messiah continually renews faith and love.

The members of the Jerusalem Community must endure plenty of attacks, but they enjoy multiple blessings. Unemployment is growing now that the cost of living has soared, and many of them were in extreme poverty, but God, who knows the needs of his children, miraculously gave them the nourishment and clothing they needed; for this he used our friends with loving hearts from different countries. The needy of our Community were aided materially as well as spiritually thanks to their prayers.

They brought us the comfort of their prayers, and to those of our Community who were in need, they gave such considerable material aid that enough remained left over to help some neighbours and friends in need.

MESSIANIC JEWISH IMMIGRATION

At the edges of Jerusalem, along the border, one can find a large *Ma'bara* (immigrant camp) that is home to 14,000 souls, originating from Persia, Iraq, Morocco, Kurdistan, Yemen, as well as from a few western countries. In view of the surrounding hills, this camp appears as a monstrous eyesore rising from the earth to spread out its shacks made of silvery gray aluminium, of brown wood, or of whitened concrete all along the valley and even on the hillsides.

Among the inhabitants of this camp is a Danish family that arrived here three years ago. The father, mother, and four children—three of whom were born in the camp—live together in a small room in one of these shacks. The lack of privacy with extremely primitive beings, filled by a strange spirit, is for them a painful trial. However, they find the spiritual light in spite of their sufferings, disappointments, and the trials they must face. This light is the Messiah, and they are a part of the Messianic Community of Israel. Some other new immigrants are also a part of this Community.

Each member of the Community comes from a different country: Germany, Austria, Bulgaria, Romania, Poland, Holland, Denmark, the United States, Russia, and Israel are their countries of origin. Each one had to go through the exile, each one has lived the tragic destiny of the Jews, each one was forced to follow the path that was destined for him without knowing the reason or purpose.

The problem that occupies Israel at this current hour, that is, the uniting of all those who were dispersed for such a long time, has found its solution in the Community. A spirit of love has overcome all the obstacles raised by the various national influences, opposing cultures, diversity of languages, temperaments, and education. The unification could only have been realised by a communal faith and complete surrender to him who is the only One who can keep us united—our Messiah.

Nevertheless, each member of the Community is but a weak and disabled man living in the most difficult and miserable conditions that are present everywhere. The temptations are great, and spirits are more and more put to the test. Without the grace of God, the protection of the Messiah, and the prayers of our friends, no one would remain upright.

We see how the prayers have been granted, how God has given us strength and harmony. It is with joy and gratitude that we can see how God has guided and blessed us. We ask that God would use us more still to be witnesses of the Messiah in Israel, and that he would open the path to us that would allow us to bring our message once again to many souls whose hearts he has prepared to receive the Messiah.

The Jewish people who left Egypt under the guidance of Moses had to be prepared by God for the task that awaited them in the promised land; likewise, the people who now return from the exile must be prepared by God for the return of the Messiah.

CHAPTER FIFTEEN
PROMISE AND FULFILMENT

I returned to Israel at the beginning of 1953 after an absence of more than three years. When I was leaving the country at the end of 1949, massive immigrations had only just begun. Since then, 800,000 Jews have immigrated to Israel.

THE RETURN

All these immigrants have come from seventy-four different countries, from the north and the south, from the east and the west; natives of the most primitive regions, as well as from the most sophisticated countries, each group bringing with it the language, customs, and practices of the countries in which they lived throughout the centuries. The peoples with whom they lived were never able to assimilate them completely, but these different environments considerably influenced their way of life.

These 800,000 new-comers were dressed, fed, housed, educated, trained in their work, and transformed into responsible Israeli citizens. An admirable task!

THE IMPOSSIBLE MADE POSSIBLE

Those who have contemplated this huge undertaking from a rational point of view have predicted disaster and the fall of the State; indeed the burden and the responsibility that such a massive immigration represents in so small and so young a State—with its multiple problems, its poverty, and its uncertain "peace"—would make it seem an impossible task to accomplish.

However, let us remember the entire history of the Jewish people: In every instance we see that the impossible is made possible; it is the demonstration of a power acting alongside Israel that greatly surpasses human reasoning and strength. In other words, it is a history that shows us the power of God acting within and through the Jewish people.

I saw this divine power bring about, in 1948, the victory that allowed for the establishment of the State of Israel, and that, in 1953, established the exiles in the promised land.

TRANSFORMATION

The tents of the first immigrant camps were, little by little, replaced by wooden or aluminium shacks. From these camps the immigrants were transferred into agricultural communities (*kibbutzim*), as well as into apartments or houses in large cities or villages.

Approximately four hundred agricultural communities have been founded since 1948, and their number continues to grow. The speed of Israel's development is almost unbelievable.

Thousands of housing projects have been spread throughout the country; these are agricultural communities, villages, or the beginnings of cities. These towns absorbed within four and a half years nearly all 800,000 immigrants. Only a relatively small percentage remained in the camps.

From the north to the south, regions that were once desolate are now inhabited, and this land that was once a barren desert has become a fertile land. Millions of trees have been planted, transforming the burnt and arid landscape into verdant countryside.

When the traveller journeys through Israel, he learns that a particular agricultural community that he has seen along the way is home to Jews originating from Turkey, and another one Jews from America or Bulgaria, from India, Morocco, South Africa, Hungary, etc. All the countries are represented. For the first time since their dispersion, nearly two thousand years ago, the Jewish people have been regathered from all countries to their own land. In this way the prophecy of Ezekiel is fulfilled before our eyes:

> Behold, I will take the people of Israel from the nations among which they have gone, and will gather them from all around, and bring them to their own land. (Ezekiel 37:21)

THE NEGEV

The most impressive changes that we find are in the Negev, that great desert region of the south. There, where throughout the centuries one could not find the faintest trace of vegetation due to the intense heat of the sun and the lack of water, green fields are now spread throughout.

For this reason pipes were installed carrying water from very far away; wells were reopened and unexpected subterranean sources were recently discovered, which allow for the usage of large quantities of water.

The subsoil of this region proved to be equally as rich, and several factories have now already been established in the Negev. A few days before my departure a very important event took place: the opening of the road from Sedom (the biblical Sodom). This road, the first that crosses the rocky mountains, ends to the southernmost part of the Dead Sea, where one finds an important potash factory. The previous factory, located at the other end of the Dead Sea, was destroyed during the Jewish-Arab war; being in Arab territory, it is actually inaccessible to Jews. The new road from Sedom opens some great possibilities in Israel.

Further south a road joins Eilat, the port of the Red Sea. In the time of Solomon, this city was known by the name of Ezion-Geber, where "King Solomon built a fleet of ships." This port once more became an important area and will be used more and more for importing the necessary equipment for the development of the Negev.

Be'er Sheva is also being rebuilt, and the primitive village is becoming more and more of an expansive city that promises to become the industrial and cultural centre of the Negev, becoming as important as Tel Aviv.

THE CITIES

Tel Aviv, Jerusalem, and Haifa spread out their hundreds of buildings over the widest areas. Houses for living in, blocks of apartments, factories, schools, and public buildings have been built in such a short period of time that the most familiar places have suddenly become unrecognisable.

The population of these cities is very mixed—ranging from easterners with dark skin to Scandinavians with blond hair and blue eyes. The more primitive and backward populations are mixing with intellectuals who have the finest education. On the main streets the prophecy of Jeremiah is realised (31:8):

> Behold, I will bring them from the north country, and
> gather them from the coasts of the earth, and with them
> the blind and the lame, the woman with child.

In the cities, one can powerfully feel the spiritual forces that dominate this great mixture of peoples, in Jerusalem in particular, in which the majority of the population originates from the east. This influence is demonstrated, for example, in the obligation of all city occupants to lock their doors at night and to avoid all trouble by never going out alone after nightfall. Prior to the massive arrival of immigrants, such precautions were unnecessary in Jerusalem.

THE FULFILLMENT

During the exile the Jews have always believed that God would fulfil his promise to regather them to their land. In their prayers they always requested the rebuilding of Jerusalem and in their heart they preserved that longing to return. However, not all those who came to Israel came with this faith or this gratitude toward God who kept his promise. Many were forced to come here because of events that took place in their country of origin, and many desired to go back there; in fact, several of them did. But, whatever the reason for their return, whether it was because of their faith, their plans, or their understanding, the Word of God that was once addressed to the prophets was fulfilled. Some events have taken place today that were predicted almost three thousand years ago.

Only the will of God has permitted the establishment of the State of Israel and the gathering of the dispersed Jews in order to plant them in the promised land. But the last chapter of their salvation is yet to be realised.

The first part of the promise now being accomplished, we can not be far from the realisation of the last chapter of the promise:

> A new heart also will I give you … I will put my spirit within you … and ye shall be my people, and I will be your God.

THE SPIRITUAL SITUATION

There is much confusion, many conflicts, and divisions in the spiritual realm. Therein Satan exercises his control and seeks to destroy those who begin to grow. Nevertheless, even in this realm one can already see the beginning of the fulfillment of the promise that will result in the return of the Messiah and the commencement of the Millennial Kingdom.

Extremist Orthodox Judaism has lost its hold on the younger generation, which follows different lines of thought. Liberal Judaism cannot satisfy the hearts of those who are searching. The conflict continues amongst all those who are separated by the different nuances of their faith.

In the Diaspora the ancient traditions, talmudic laws, and faith in the divine promises united the Jews and gave them the strength to resist all efforts of assimilation attempted by the other peoples amongst whom they were dispersed.

In our day, however, the circumstances have changed. They have returned to their own country where one may find all the different schools of thought and all levels of faith, free from the danger of assimilation by other peoples and other beliefs, and they must now face a new situation.

THE NEW TESTAMENT

In the Diaspora, the reading of the New Testament was forbidden in most Jewish families. Generally, Jews did not truly know the principles of Christianity and they were deeply marked by the persecutions and the hatred that they were subjected to by those who called themselves Christians in Christian countries.

However, today we are seeing a new interest in the New Testament in the State of Israel. Bibles and New Testaments in all languages pour into the country. We have been told that those who spread the New Testament here encounter very little opposition, and we can clearly see the signs of interest in the gospel of Messiah growing.

In certain schools they read the New Testament in literature class, but it is still not spoken of as being the way of salvation. It is, however, a means for making known the message of the New Testament to the Jewish people directly, who are thus prepared for the day when their understanding shall be clear and when they shall receive the message of Yeshua and recognise him as the Messiah.

The Christian citizens have complete freedom of religion in Israel, but the Christian missionary work is disapproved of. It is difficult to erase the impression made by certain missionaries who, in the sincerity of their efforts, did not know how to approach the Jews and they stirred up an antagonism that translated into the creation of an organisation charged with combating every missionary influence among the Jews.

THE MESSIANIC COMMUNITY IN ISRAEL

We have seen the power of God manifested in Israel in a way that cannot be ignored: the founding of the State, the regathering of the exiles dispersed in all countries, their establishment in the promised land, and the preparation for their spiritual revival.

In the Messianic Community of Jerusalem, we still see other effects of God's work among his people Israel. This small group of believing Jews, also having come from different countries and established in Jerusalem, testifies that the grace of God is returning upon Israel; we see in these few Jews that which will be the final destiny of the entire Jewish people: All will realise and recognise that Yeshua of Nazareth is Messiah and King.

For seven years this Community that was created, guided, and protected by the Messiah has been used as a spiritual centre in Jerusalem. Its members suffer the same material difficulties and the same ordeals as the other Israelis and, even though the government causes each difficulty, they suffer more and more individual spiritual attacks that are more serious and more difficult to repel than an overt attack.

Another spiritual centre was created in Haifa, where the lights of the Sabbath are illuminated each week.

The message of the Messiah is proclaimed among numerous Jews by Rabbi Daniel Zion, who, after having been excluded from the synagogue, gave open lectures and could, in so doing, address certain Jews and proclaim that Yeshua is the Messiah of the Jews. The faithful who no longer had the right to hear him within the walls of the synagogue could now listen to his message outside of its enclosure.

The message of the kingdom is now proclaimed amongst the Jews in Israel, and no power will be able to prevent it.

The Community in Jerusalem, although small and in no way spectacular, is the spiritual centre of a worldwide movement. All those who visit it from the different countries they inhabit establish a personal link between Jerusalem and the centres for prayer that exist in the entire world.

This Community, the first sign of a spiritual revival in Israel, was planted in Jerusalem seven years ago, like a tiny mustard seed in the shade of lush vegetation. And we already see its branches extend in all the countries of the world, gathering the believers into one larger Brotherhood—the Jewish Christian Brotherhood of the kingdom, in the same vision of the Messianic Kingdom.

This Brotherhood that covers the world surrounds the small Messianic Community of Israel in a circle of light, sustaining it with its prayers and in so doing making it possible for it to withstand the daily trials that beat down upon its members and which will come increasingly in number with the nearing of the end of this period.

A stream of blessings connects the Jerusalem centre on both sides to all the places in the world where this Brotherhood reaches. God is not only regathering the Jewish people, but all the Christians of all countries. The Messianic Kingdom, promised so long ago, is already almost visible. But the dark days that must precede it draw near, and they do so quickly. We have shown rays of light in the darkness of our era, but let us not be deceived by the blackness, cleverness, and the subtlety of the satanic power.

THE DANGERS

Satan holds power in the government of Israel. He influences politics, religion, and education. He has a foothold in all areas. He has interests in all the affairs of the State of Israel. But that which interests him most of all is the Messianic Community, those who display the banner of the Messiah, for that banner carries his condemnation.

This is why this small Community in Jerusalem is the main target of his attacks; this is why it has had to go through one crisis after another during the seven years of its existence.

We must face a new crisis; Satan tries at all cost to individually break the members who form the Community. He uses all possible means and we know that his tricks can deceive even the elected.

The dangers we face in these constant attacks of the Adversary force us to constantly remain vigilant—we not only exercise this vigilance within ourselves, but we must equally watch over all those around us and be prudent even toward those who are the closest and most dear to us, for Satan uses all means and he certainly knows our weaknesses and our most personal failings. If the enemy we confront is recognisable as an enemy, the battle is easy. But if the enemy attacks us by surprise and under disguise, we risk falling prey to the ambush.

Today Satan uses all forms of disguise to try to annihilate the children of light, and what better disguise is there than an angel of light? In our Community as well he has appeared in this disguise—an angel of light—and beneath this mask he tries to destroy the Community from within. It is therefore necessary to constantly purify it. It is not the number that counts, nor the progress that it seems to have made in spreading the message, but the heart and the faith of those few members who form its core, those who carry the banner of the King whom they await.

They must completely surrender in his hands; they must be ready to leave home, father, mother, husband, wife, child, every earthly possession, every personal tie, to carry the banner into the darkness of night, eyes fixed on the star that guides them to the dawn of a new day.

The dangers that threaten us are not the shadows, but the powers of the shadows in their disguise as angels of light. Many lights shine in the shadows of our age, some lights oftentimes very brilliant—so brilliant that it is difficult to perceive the stars. If we walk at night in the streets of a capital city, such as London or Paris for example, everywhere there are lights that draw our attention to the pleasures of this world. These lights are dazzling, even blinding, and once one is surrounded by them, who would then think to raise his eyes to look at the feeble glow of the stars? How dull and small they appear!

There are also some of these artificial lights spiritually that divert our glance from the heavenly star that must guide us. There are some of these lights of which we must be cautious; for us they are a warning: let us be especially vigilant so that we are not led astray by them, and let us not lose sight of the heavenly star.

May we be vigilant, remain calm, follow the star with our eyes that leads us to Jerusalem, and when the lights of this world are extinguished, the brilliant morning star will rise above the Holy City.

We rejoice in seeing the divine hand at work in Israel and we look to Jerusalem where streams of blessings flow for the entire world. "For out of Zion shall go forth the law, and the Word of the LORD from Jerusalem."

CHAPTER SIXTEEN

MESSAGE FOR THE CONSECRATION OF THE SANCTUARY

When, at Hanukkah (1954), you gather for the consecration of the new centre of our community, I will be united with you in spirit and in prayer, and I will request divine blessings for the new sanctuary and for all those who will gather there.

It was during Hanukkah, in 1948, that the first home of our Community in Jerusalem was consecrated, on the Street of the Prophets. The light of Messiah was, for the first time, lit on the Mount of Olives, and then in different locations until God gifted us with this sanctuary, the "Upper Room" where the light can now be lit in peace.

All those who have taken care of this light have had much to suffer and plenty of trials and difficulties to overcome, and all those who gather around this light have had to face numerous dangers and great difficulties. But God held his protective hand over the sanctuary of the "Upper Room," and he blessed all those who came to pray by showing them what this light signified in Israel.

This light that we kindle each Friday evening to the glory of Yeshua our Saviour is a guiding star for all those who await his return as King of Israel; and not only in Israel, but in numerous other countries. The prayers of the faithful souls have risen toward God continually for the protection and the blessing of the new sanctuary, and God answered them. A guard of angels surrounded the "Upper Room" on the Street of the Prophets, and those of the community who guarded it faithfully enjoyed great favour.

This period has now come to an end—a new home and a new sanctuary will be inaugurated. I have read with profound joy how the spirit of love and fellowship is evident among you and how you have contributed to making this sanctuary so beautiful.

We have earnestly prayed in London and in other places that God would bless and guide everything that concerns this new centre. God has chosen the guardians of this new home; it is a great privilege that brings with it numerous blessings. May the light of the Messiah, that shines brightly in your hearts, make you powerful witnesses of your faith and make you faithful to your calling.

This inauguration that is taking place at Hanukkah coincides well with this festival of lights—a reminder of the light that continued to shine, even though throughout the eight days the vial of oil was insufficient for keeping it sustained. It is good that we should remember that it is not *ours*, the vial of oil that sustains the light, rather it is the supply of the Holy Spirit.

May the light be rekindled in your hearts each time you kindle the light of Hanukkah and of the Sabbath, and may this ceremony remind you of the birth of the Light of the World. May the Holy Spirit enter you all the more until your light may shine with the greatest brilliance!

Do not fear the dangers that surround you, even if you find yourselves at the border of enemy territories. God has always protected his Sanctuary and kept aglow the light of the Saviour throughout all dangers. If the dangers increase, may he reinforce his protection. Our prayers for you rise incessantly toward God, and his watch rests continually upon us. Wherever the light of the Saviour shines in Israel, he establishes his bastion. Look to him always; he will guide you, protect you, and bless you. He will give you power, joy, and peace. He will use you as conduits of light and love to shine light in the dark shadows around you.

> For, behold, the darkness shall cover the earth, and gross darkness the people: but the LORD shall arise upon thee, and his glory shall be seen upon thee. (Isaiah 60:2)

CHAPTER SEVENTEEN

FEAR NOT!

SPEECH AT THE CONFERENCE OF
10 OCTOBER 1954 IN LONDON

When we were reunited together for our last conference we did not yet know what 1954 had in store for us. Now, the grace of God has permitted us to reunite again, so that we would be strengthened in our spiritual unity and so that we would better understand the message for our time.

Not only the biblical prophecy, but the newspaper articles also show us the importance of the year 1954. It is a decisive year in the history of humanity. If we remember the beginning of our history, Adam and Eve, we feel ourselves connected to them more than ever before. It is only now that we are able to truly realise the significance of a humanity succumbing to the influence of Satan, to the temptation of eating of the tree of knowledge. It is in this year, 1954, that we are experiencing the consequences of the first disobedience to God. Men now have the ability and power to destroy every living thing and the entire planet with the H bomb. They have that power as long as the earth resides under the dominion of Satan. Without Messiah there will be no hope for the entire world. The leaders of nations meet with each other again and again but they never find solutions to their problems. The only result is an increase in preparations for war. We live in unusually climactic and troubled conditions, with illnesses and mysterious causes of death, with earthquakes and floods. Each day brings us a new catastrophe and we do not know what will happen here at the end of the year.

Learned men consider flying saucers as objects not created by men and whose characteristics are beyond all human possibility. Even the most courageous men become frightened upon coming in contact with flying saucers. It appears that not only the earth but also the spheres of other planets are troubled.

KNOWLEDGE AND FEAR

Man was afraid for the first time after having eaten from the tree of knowledge. When God created man in his own image and gave him the Garden of Eden, man had no inkling of fear. God, in his love and wisdom, prepared for him everything that he needed. God walked with him and spoke with him and he saw God's splendor. It was only after eating of the forbidden fruit that Adam and Eve hid themselves behind trees because they were afraid when the LORD called to them. Concurrent with the increase in knowledge, fear grew. Today, with man having a knowledge that is greater than ever, fear is also overwhelmingly greater.

These are sure signs that the return of the Lord is near. Humanity is captive in the nets that Satan has woven for it. It has no means by which to control the destruction. We are in the darkest hour. Fear and power give rise to most of the thoughts and actions of man. Without Messiah, there is every reason to fear.

THE TIME OF THE END

Let us ask ourselves if we, who are also Christians, are afraid! I believe that fear reigns in numerous Christian hearts. Several people say that we must not speak or write of the distresses that surround us, only of the pleasant things. We must close our eyes to the terrors and the still worse things that are to come. Others believe that we are not destined to endure the tribulations to come because we will be taken up beforehand.

Let us listen to the words of Yeshua the Messiah. When his disciples asked him what would be the sign of the end, he responded to them:

> Wars and rumours of wars, a people will rise up against another people, famines, pestilence, and earthquakes. But all this will only be the beginning. You will be persecuted, killed, and hated because of my name. You will betray each other and detest one another, and false prophets will arise and they will deceive many. Stars will fall from the sky; the heavenly powers will be shaken and men will die of fright.

These words of Yeshua the Messiah are for us today, for we are in the time of which he speaks. We are coming to see some of these events and we await for everything to occur in accordance with his word, for he says: "These things must come, all this must occur." He does not say that we will escape these things, rather that "those who withstand until the end will be saved."

Yeshua the Messiah did not withhold anything from his disciples when speaking to them of the tribulations and the time of the end. The disciples expected them in their lifetime. Must we then conceal these things from ourselves and try to escape them? Must we be afraid because of this? "For God hath not given us the spirit of fear; but of power, and of love, and of a sound mind."

THE NARROW PATH

Until Messiah's return, the earth remains under the dominion of Satan. This is why men carry out abominable things before our eyes. The earth is covered in shadows, but a narrow path leads through the shadows to the light. Messiah has opened it to us and it leads to the Messianic Kingdom. Our thoughts are inspired for us; the evil ones by Satan and the good ones, the thoughts of love, by God. The true Christians who walk on the path of light are inspired by the Holy Spirit. It is only when Satan is bound that his inspirations will cease. Then the Holy Spirit will guide all of humanity. But until that moment, Satan's influence will increase more and more.

DO NOT ALLOW YOURSELVES TO BE DECEIVED

If we accept the message of Messiah and the Holy Spirit guides us, we will understand the events that encircle us and not be led astray. When Yeshua the Messiah spoke of the signs of the time of the end he initially said: "Take heed that no man deceive you." False prophets will arise and perform miracles—do not allow yourselves to be deceived.

The false prophets will always speak of peace in order to conceal their dark actions, and those who are fearful will always be prepared to listen to them. He who attempts to escape the tribulations is allowing himself to be deceived by these talks of peace. The antichrist will be the greatest of all the false prophets and the world will be so happy about the promises of peace that it will hear from him. It will follow him and serve him until the day when his duplicity will be made evident.

Yeshua the Messiah tells us to beware of the tribulations and the deceptions that are coming, but he also shows us the path on which we will be protected from all need and all danger. The only way, the path of light, is love. Satan controls all things except love. Only love can triumph in the battle against Satan. If we fight him with any other means we will fail. He is powerless against love. We must be armoured with love. He who is not filled with love will in the end fail. Be on guard: the love must not turn cold. "He who withstands until the end will be saved." Only he in whom love is not turned cold shall remain until the end, on the path of light that leads to the kingdom.

Such is the Word of God, the message that the LORD has given us for our time. If we say that we believe in God and we have fear in our hearts, we deceive ourselves and we allow ourselves to be easily deceived. Fear is weakness in faith. God says to his people, "Fear not, for I am with you," and Paul writes to Timothy that "perfect love is fearless."[18] May we have the wisdom to understand all that occurs today around us in the world. May we be prepared for the gravest events that are coming, that our hearts would be so filled with love that we would be sure that God is with us—for God is love. And if God is with us, then whom should we fear? God has not given us a spirit of timidity but a spirit of strength, love, and wisdom, and as a result we can say to anyone who wishes to listen to us: "Fear not, do not move, and see how God will save you."

---

[18] [Perhaps a paraphrase of 1 John 4:18, which says, "Perfect love casts out all fear."]

CHAPTER EIGHTEEN

COMMUNION IN THE HOLY SPIRIT

An excerpt from a letter to a friend who is searching for a community that is enlivened by the Holy Spirit.

W hy is there still not communion in the Holy Spirit?" you ask. Well, because those who have heard the call to build it have not wanted to humble themselves before God and do that which was expected of them. Everyone expects to take and not to give. This is why they were disappointed, as you are, losing their faith and patience from waiting on God.

GIVE OR TAKE?

If we always wait for others to do what is necessary, then we will never have communion in the Holy Spirit, but we shall, only when we search our hearts, realising our own standing before God, and permit the Holy Spirit to work in us. The communion must begin in our hearts. Neither time for meditation nor Bible studies can help us in this if our daily work and our relationships with our fellow men do not compel us to search our own hearts. We will not have peace with God unless we abandon all of our prejudices, our personal desires, and our demanding natures.

Our burden is so heavy that it can be alleviated only in carrying the burdens of others; the fatigue of our feet can only be eased in washing the feet of others.

Our own problems will be resolved only if we attach ourselves to those of our companions. Then we will be conduits of love and the Holy Spirit will heal us and strengthen us by the measure in which it flows through us.

GRACE

We have received immeasurable grace, not in order to guard it for ourselves, but in order to spread it. If we want to guard the grace of God only for ourselves, we will soon lose it, whereas if we share it, we will receive much more.

If we accomplish that which God desires now, we will receive much greater blessings than we can even imagine later on, for the LORD has promised to pour out more blessings than any container could hold.

This is not dependent upon the work. More important is the spirit in which we perform it. If we perform each one of our tasks in the Spirit of Messiah, even if they repulse us, all the scaffoldings of oppositions that surround us will collapse. Pray that God would give you the strength to work in this spirit, and you will see miracles occur.

Before us always stands that which Messiah, in his unspeakable love and his tireless patience, has accomplished for our benefit, beyond our comprehension. We also must not believe that we could, on our part, deprive ourselves of it by our own selfish desires. And yet this is precisely what we often repeat. We will never be able to grasp why grace is extended to us to take part as heralds and propagators of the movement of preparation for his reign.

SOLDIERS

I also believe that you are called to become part of this army, and when you are fully aware of your own status, you will prosper in your relationships with the people with whom you are associated, possessing more clarity and prudence.

As a soldier of Messiah we are called to lead the fight of light against the shadows. The power of the Enemy is considerable, and we have no means of defence against his attacks. But our Leader equips us with a secret weapon against which all the armies of the Adversary are powerless. This invincible and victorious weapon is "LOVE," a love with no reservation. Every combatant in the army of Messiah must be equipped with this weapon when he opposes the enemy on the battlefield.

As an active soldier we are not to expect an easy and comfortable life. We must accept the stakes of combat at any moment and obey every command. Victory is assured, but the battle is always underway and, above all, we must not slacken.

BUILDERS

More than our soldierly duties, we also have the duty of building. We must build small refuges of light and shelters for the weak, the wounded, and the elderly. Just as the battle cannot be conducted in isolation, so too, these refuges cannot be created by someone who is isolated.

We must work as a team, and yet each person is given a precise mission. The work cannot be commenced unless everyone acts in the harmony of one spirit alone: the Holy Spirit.

It is not possible by human estimation to build such a community, but we have a Leader who sends us the directives and the power to successfully complete this work. However, these directives can be followed only if each person uses the secret weapon of love, an unconditional love.

If we are to prepare the path of the kingdom, to make the signs that lead to the light, to establish communities by the Holy Spirit, then there is no other path by which to obtain these results other than to unconditionally abandon our lives to our Leader and King so that he can make us conduits of his love.

ON THE WAY

All of us ardently desire the kingdom of Messiah. We look for all the signs and we hope to find them in each person whom we encounter. We expect to find the love promised for the kingdom in all those whom Messiah has called to prepare the path of his reign, and we think that we will find in them the true communion of the Holy Spirit. This is how deceptions then arrive because we find in them the same weaknesses and the same lack of love that we have recognised in ourselves.

We must admit that we are not yet perfect, and we are all called to continue to work, no less than those around us.

We are not yet in the kingdom, but only on the path that leads to it.

Others of us, soldiers and builders, have the duty of obeying the King, and we must relinquish the direction of the battle and the plan for the building into the hands of our Master. It is just as forbidden for us to complain as it is to criticise our companions, to give advice to our Leader as it is to go ahead prematurely. How good it will be if we are able to accomplish the duties that are incumbent upon us.

STONES FOR BUILDING

If we are given stones for building that are difficult to smoothen and not as we would have hoped, we must also think that our Master certainly knew the precise reason he gave them to us to fashion.

He has the entire plan of the building in mind, but we are not capable of seeing it in its vast immensity, nor do we comprehend it. We must accept every piece that he gives us as a precious gift, even if it is the most insignificant raw material, and give thanks day and night to our Master for the right that he grants us to the privilege of having been called to participate in his work.

But then we will be disappointed by other people because we expect to receive from them precisely that which we must give to them: unconditional love. We are disappointed because they do not understand us, because they do not act as we do, and they do not behave as we would expect; in short, it is because we forget that they have the same flaws as we do. The only remedy for entering into communion with those whom God places beside us is to turn the image around and recognise in ourselves that which disappoints us in others. Then we have much to do to conquer these things within ourselves, for we no longer have any more time to observe the "speck in our brother's eye."

BEACON

We have, as soldiers of Messiah, the duty to be conduits of absolute love. The halos of light that he created in this world of shadows are like beacons that he has illuminated so that we, who are the guardians, could keep them aglow by the reserves of oil sealed in him, by an absolute love. If this oil runs out, the light will be obscured, and exhausted pilgrims on the path of the kingdom will get lost in the shadows.

May we always be concerned enough to make sure the oil does not run out, but if the time comes when our fellow is lacking it, we must give him twice as much. If, on the contrary, we should begin to complain that our fellow is lacking, our reserve could run dry and our task be gravely damaged.

Our Master demands a total obedience: "If someone wants to follow me, let him deny himself and let him take up his cross; then he may follow me." Such a man will be filled to the utmost with love and kindness. "There is no greater love than for a man to give his life for his friends."

Messiah knows all of our weaknesses and has been tempted in the same manner as we:

> He will not permit you to be tempted beyond your ability,
> but with each trial He gives you the means of escape so
> that you will be able to withstand it.

If we encounter difficulties that are seemingly impossible to overcome, when our weaknesses are so great that we cannot bear them, then may we recall that "we can do all things through him who strengthens us." It is only with him and through him that we can commune in the Holy Spirit.

CHAPTER NINETEEN

JEWISH CHRISTIAN BROTHERHOOD OF THE KINGDOM

The second Messianic Jewish Conference in Basle took place on Sunday, January 27, 1952. The hall, seating five hundred people, was soon filled to capacity. Many were unable to enter for lack of space.

However, notwithstanding the overcrowding, there was an orderliness and quietness that expressed the earnestness of those who attended the conference, fully conscious of the importance of the occasion.

Friends from all parts of Switzerland were present, as well as from France, Germany, and England.

The spirit of unity and harmony was maintained undisturbed throughout the conference. If the "adversary" had representatives in the hall that day, they had no power even to raise a voice or make a sign.

It was decided that a committee of twelve should be formed to represent France, Germany, England, and Switzerland. Three delegates from each country are to be elected in their own circles, with the power to co-opt other members. The name suggested by Abram Poljak for this International Brotherhood was "The Brotherhood of the Kingdom" as the movement in Europe is made up mainly of Gentile Christians.

This suggestion was put to the vote and defeated by an overwhelming majority in favour of "*Jewish Christian* Brotherhood of the Kingdom". Thus the International Movement was founded and named at this second conference in Basle.

It is hoped that this new step taken will be a means of linking up all who are called to this work, that they may go forward together, strengthened and empowered by the spirit of Messiah, to proclaim the message of the kingdom in all countries.

MESSIANIC JEWS AND GENTILES

It was my privilege to be present at the conference in Basle as a representative of the London Community, and to meet many of our friends in Switzerland. I was deeply impressed by the fervour of the response to the call of the Messianic Jewish Community, the great interest and support of the work by the Gentile Christian brethren, and the unity in spirit.

The vision of the kingdom of Israel, and the mission of the Messianic Jewish community to prepare the way that leads to the kingdom, has called out of all nations, churches, and sects, those who have been chosen by God to herald the second coming of the Messiah Yeshua, and to proclaim his approaching kingdom in Israel.

At this conference in Basle, friends and supporters from many countries were present. They had come from various circles of Christian believers, from different countries, different walks of life, but there was one spirit uniting them all—the spirit of Messiah. At this meeting, where almost seven hundred people filled the hall, there was peace and harmony, unity in spirit, vision and purpose; an earnest desire to serve God, proclaim his kingdom, and serve one another in love, tolerance, and humility.

The success of the conference was the result of much preparation in prayer. In Jerusalem, England, France, Germany, and Switzerland, so many faithful and trusting hearts had been lifted up in prayer to God asking for his guidance and blessing upon the meeting. Those prayers had been answered by a pouring out of the

Spirit upon all who delivered the messages and those who were ready to receive them. It was an important day in the history of the development of the work of the Messianic Jewish Community.

Now that the International Brotherhood has been founded, it is hoped that members and friends in all countries may have opportunities of meeting from time to time, at conferences in different towns, thus linking up in the work, that the message of the kingdom may be carried to all corners of the earth.

BRIDGE TO THE KINGDOM

As Jews and Gentiles, one in Messiah, with strengthened faith and vision cleared, we are called to prepare the way of the Lord. We stand on the bridge that crosses from one aeon to another, we must support and uphold one another until the bridge is crossed and the new era, the kingdom of the Messiah, will be established on earth.

Step by step God will lead us, if we answer his call without hesitation, without doubt, without thought for ourselves. Two things are necessary in this joint work of Jew and Gentile during this period of transition, this crossing of the bridge—prayer and a united spirit, the spirit of love, which overcomes all obstacles, which is the assurance we have that the Messiah is in our midst, that he is leading us, guiding our footsteps toward his kingdom.

Only by the manifestation of the spirit of Messiah in the personal life of each one of us can we be known. We will not be known by a name—only by love. People will see us, hear us, look at us, come to us according as love flows through us into the world. No names, words, teaching, or preaching alone will prepare the way for Messiah. Love and love only can do this work.

CHAPTER TWENTY

THE CONFERENCE
IN STRASBOURG

The International Conference of the Jewish Christian Brotherhood of the Kingdom, founded at the Basle Conference in January, 1952, took place in Strasbourg on Whit-Sunday [Pentecost], June 1, 1952. Delegates were present from five countries—England, Germany, France, Switzerland, and Israel. About four hundred people attended.

On Sunday morning the conference began at 10 o'clock with a closed meeting attended by over one hundred friends from the different countries.

Abram Poljak gave an address on Matthew 24, verse 14—"And this gospel of the kingdom shall be preached in all the world for a witness to all nations; and then shall the end come," showing thereby that our mission is to carry the message of the kingdom into all corners of the earth; reminding us also that the time is short and that the night, in which no man can work, is very near.

Then the following resolutions were put to the meeting to be agreed upon by vote:

1. To increase the membership of the International Committee formed at the Basle Conference, where it was decided to elect three delegates from each of the four countries—France, England, Germany, Switzerland.

2. To form a secretarial centre in each country to contact and correspond with friends in other countries of the same language, thus strengthening and coordinating the work in all lands.

3. To make Jerusalem the centre of the International Movement.

4. To elect a Chairman for the Jewish Christian Brotherhood of the Kingdom, nominating Albert Springer of Jerusalem to fill that position.

5. To prepare a future conference in Jerusalem with representatives from all countries.

These resolutions were accepted unanimously, manifesting the unity of spirit and common vision of all present.

It was also decided to form a prayer league through which there would be an interchange of intercessions and a strengthening of the spiritual bonds.

The conference ended after a day of complete harmony and unity, where differences of language, nationality, and background were overcome by the spirit of love and the common vision of the approaching kingdom.

CONFERENCE FOR THE KINGDOM

There have been many historical conferences of world importance in Strasbourg, conferences with high aims and ideals, having the peace of the world as their goal, but they failed because their foundation was only human goodwill. The only lasting and enduring peace for humanity and the world will come when the Author of Peace, the King of Kings returns to set up his kingdom.

This kingdom will be established on earth at God's appointed time. To some the grace has been given to have this vision, and to know the King, our Lord and Messiah. To others this grace has not been give; but whether we can discern it or not the plan of God proceeds toward its goal. For thousands of years believers have waited for the kingdom; some with faith that never wavered;

others weakened by disappointment when the expected hour did not come. For long it was only the vision that kept faith strong, but today we can see many signs manifesting the nearness of the establishment of the kingdom, and one of these is the conference that took place in Strasbourg on June 1.

JEWISH CHRISTIAN BROTHERHOOD OF THE KINGDOM

This International Movement—the Jewish Christian Brotherhood of the Kingdom—was founded in Basle this year; the Strasbourg Conference marks another milestone. Before the end of this age "the gospel of the kingdom must be preached unto all nations." Already our publications in English, French, and German have reached readers in thirty-six countries: Switzerland, Germany, Austria, Sweden, Norway, Denmark, Finland, France, Belgium, Holland, Britain, Ireland, Italy, United States of America, Canada, Newfoundland, British West Indies, Dutch West Indies, Argentine, Brazil, Chile, Guiana, Australia, New Zealand, South Africa, Nigeria, French Equatorial Africa, French West Africa, Korea, Indo-China, Indonesia, India, Iraq, Israel, Turkey, Persia. Articles taken from our journals have been published in different magazines and translated into other languages. A missionary in a remote part of central Africa has even translated our message into the native language of the tribes to whom he ministers.

Thus we see how quickly the message is being spread, and it is the task of the International Movement to strengthen the ties that unite those who have been chosen and called by God in all countries of the world, those who one day will be "pillars" in the kingdom of God.

NEXT YEAR IN JERUSALEM

At this conference in Strasbourg, five countries were represented, three languages were spoken. We look ahead to the time when all countries will be represented and many more languages spoken. It may be that when the time comes, the gift of tongues will again be given to us. However, the language of the Spirit—of love—will supersede all other languages, as was shown at the Strasbourg conference, when many who could not understand the actual words spoken, were so completely in harmony in the Spirit that they grasped the essence of what was said.

Abram Poljak concluded the morning meeting with the final words of the Passover service—"Next year in Jerusalem." In every Jewish heart there is the longing to return to Jerusalem. In every Christian's heart there is also the longing to be in the city where the Messiah lived and will return to establish the kingdom of God.

We do not know how long it will be, but the march to Jerusalem has begun; the conference in Strasbourg is the first step in preparation for the conference in Jerusalem, and when we meet there shall we not be at the gates of the kingdom?

CHAPTER TWENTY-ONE

LOVE THY NEIGHBOUR
AS THYSELF

The greatest problem that confronts each one of us is how to live at peace with our neighbour, how to love our neighbour as ourselves. This begins with our personal relationships in the family and ends with the relationship between nation and nation, which, until now has always ended with wars.

WHO IS MY NEIGHBOUR?

"Who is our neighbour?" was the question a lawyer asked Yeshua, and the answer given him was the parable of the Good Samaritan, illustrating the one good neighbour who helped the man lying in the street in distress, and the two who crossed to the other side of the road in order to avoid helping him.

Our neighbour can be either our friend or our enemy. We are asked to love them both. It is easy to love the one who is good to us and helps us, but how can we have the same love for the one who hates us and does evil toward us? Yeshua said:

> If you love them who love you, what thank have ye? For sinners also do even the same. But love ye your enemies and do good *hoping for nothing* again, and your reward shall be great, and ye shall be the children of the Highest: for he is kind unto the unthankful and unto the evil.

From the human standpoint it is impossible to love the neighbour who hates us and does evil toward us. When treated this way we are either goaded into responsive hate and return blow for blow, or else we run away and hide our evil thoughts within ourselves. By this we show ourselves to be no better than our enemy, and certainly devoid of all neighbourly love.

Yet we are told to love our enemies and hope for nothing in return. If we want to become "children of the Highest" we must follow in the way of our Father by being "kind to the unthankful and unto the evil." To love our neighbour, to love our enemy, means being kind to the unthankful and unto the evil.

How can we do this? There is only one way to approach and find the solution to this problem—obedience to the first and most important of all the commandments:

> Thou shalt love the Lord thy God with all thy heart, and with all thy soul, and with all thy strength, and with all thy mind.

If we do this we will love our neighbour as ourselves, whether he be friend or foe.

BOTH THE EVIL AND THE GOOD

To love God means to accept willingly all things, both pleasing and painful, as coming from him, and to believe that whatever comes from him is for our good—to teach us, to make clear to us our own weakness, to reveal the darkness within us, which we recognise more easily in our neighbour, and above all, that we may understand the meaning of grace—of God's saving grace, his great love toward us.

If we were in contact only with good neighbours we would never be called upon to show mercy and forgiveness, we would never understand our own great need of God's mercy and forgiveness. Yeshua said: "woe unto you when all men shall speak well of you! For so did their fathers to the false prophets."

If our neighbour is unjust to us, speaking evil of us, taking away all that we have, striking us blow after blow, let us see that as a mirror to our own souls, and in that revelation we will see the manifestation of God's grace toward us, asking us to show the same mercy and forgiveness to our neighbour as he has shown to us.

Once we understand this it becomes possible for us to love our neighbour as ourselves. Whatever evil he may do to us, he is not our enemy, he is only a sinner the same as we are, and by grace he can become a child of the Highest, just as God has called us to be, if we show mercy, as our Father is also merciful—if we are kind to the unthankful and to the evil.

Let us not cross to the other side of the road when a neighbour lies helpless in the street, not demand justice or gratitude for what we do for our neighbour. Let us not return blow for blow, nor harbour anger or evil thoughts within us, but let us be kind to the unthankful and to the evil. Great is the reward—for then we become children of the Highest.

AT THE APPOINTED HOUR

It is sometimes very difficult to understand why certain things happen to us. We make plans and try to arrange our lives according to our desires. We expect things to proceed in the way we direct them, but so often the results are so contrary to our expectations.

We forget one important thing and that is that our lives are not directed by our own will, neither do results of our effort work out according to our way of thinking. Our lives are directed by higher powers, and when God is directing, it is not according to our way of thinking, for God's ways are not as our ways.

The Bible teaches us something of God's ways by giving illustrations of the working of his power in directing the nation of Israel. And even more revealing for us are the accounts of events in the personal lives of individual Jews.

For example, we have the story of two Jews in Jerusalem who were destined to bear witness of God's power, whose lives were directed by God. The one was a lame man, a cripple from birth. The other was a fisherman, a poor, ignorant, unlearned man. Their ways in life were very different. The one had to suffer and beg alms for his living. The other had to leave his fishing nets and follow Yeshua, and to him alone was given the greatest revelation from God—that Yeshua was the Messiah of Israel.

It would seem that there was very little connection between these two men, whose lives were so different, yet both were being prepared for a special mission at an appointed hour—one along the path of suffering, the other along a specially favoured path. Until that hour was come it was hard to understand the direction of those two lives—only God knew.

CHAPTER TWENTY-TWO
CARRY ONE ANOTHER

The word "community" has several meanings. Usually it refers to a group of people with common interests, a common mentality, or common ideals. What they possess in common are only impersonal traits.

Many such groups exist for purely carnal reasons, and are animated by worldly goals; others are inspired by grand ideals. But then there are communities that God has brought to life, which are guided by his Spirit. The people of such a group are often called together against their own will and their own desire. But God has called them together, and led them to mutual service and to be welded together in unity.

The members of such a community are to become tools of divine power; this demands the submission of their wills, their ideas, feelings, and desires, as these are often opposed to the will of God. "Your ways are not my ways," said God to his people. Man's ways do not lead to peace and happiness, yet only ever nearer to the abyss of total destruction.

Every one of us is a part of the world; in us live all the desires that govern it and direct its paths. These desires must be handed over to God, and our ways must be directed by him. When someone becomes a member of a group that God has called, the "termination process" begins.

It is a difficult and painful process. At every step it poses difficult tests. Only he who is truly willing and given over to the task can endure these tests; therefore such a community only grows slowly. Indeed, they are more likely to be smaller than larger.

THE MESSIANIC COMMUNITY

We believe that the Messianic Jewish community has been formed by God, as a group called out of Israel. It has been prepared and strengthened by him to hold up the torch of Messiah in Israel.

Most communities look up to a person who represents its ideal, and who commonly has a stronger personality than the others. He is the leader, who leads and forms the group according to his own will and vision. The Messianic Jewish community acknowledges only one leader—Yeshua the Messiah. His teaching is the only authoritative principle, and his power is the only way to conquest. We hold high the torch of his light!

A HEAVY WEIGHT

But how heavy it is to hold this torch! Before we can hold it, it must burn inside us, and lighten every nook and cranny; it must illuminate all of the carefully kept secrets that we have hidden in the dark corners of our selves.

Moses was prepared and tested for forty years before he could hold the "rod of God," and even then he could not use this power alone; he required Aaron and others to help him. As Moses stood on the mountain, while Amalek battled against his people, he had to hold up the "rod of God" without letting it fall, because when the rod was lowered, the enemy was victorious, but when it was held up, it gave Israel power over them. As Moses' arms became heavy and he could not hold the "rod of God" any longer, Aaron and Hur came to help him. They could have criticised him, taken the rod from him and held it themselves—but they came to help him, to support him.

Similarly, we learn in community to carry each other in moments of weakness, to help and with one another to fulfill the task of holding up the torch. In this unity and this common service of God we also have the power to overcome all enemies.

THE MOST DIFFICULT TEST

The Messianic Jewish community serves as a sign in Israel of the love and power of Messiah and the proclamation of his return. It is not enough to believe and preach these things. "Faith without works" is insufficient. But good works alone are also not enough: "If I give all my possessions to the poor, that would not be useful for me for anything"—if I do not have love. This love that is required of us is the only way for us to bear witness of our leader.

The most difficult test of this love is within the community. When a few people come together with natural fondness for each other and similarity of character, temperament, and origin, the test is not difficult; but in a community whose members are brought together by God and not through affection or desire, there we have the real test.

The members of the Messianic Jewish community have been called, one after another, from different countries, different professions, different ideologies. In this community there are external contrasts of temperament, character, and viewpoint; it is truly difficult to call such a colourful group to serve together. Only God can bring together such a representative group. The members are not only starkly different in their human qualities, but appear to have been chosen by God as the weakest vessels, so that in and through them his power may be made known.

Here also is the greatest test, not only for individuals and the community, but also for outsiders, who see neither saints nor heroes, but weak and helpless creatures, greater sinners than themselves.

For the members of a community the test consists of love, in which all differences and impediments are overcome in the spirit of Messiah. For the outsider it is a test of faith—faith in the power that uses weak tools, if only they are willing.

Love always stands guard over the weaknesses of others, in order to help and support them. But the enemy also watches and waits for the time when our arms become heavy and our hands tired. He looks for our weaknesses and attempts to obstruct us, and if we are alone, he can advance on us at will. Only together, when we stand by each other, help each other, and in love and unity carry each other, can we build a castle that the enemy cannot overcome.

Yeshua sent his disciples out two by two in order to spread the light of his teachings, and said, "Where two or three are gathered in my name, I am there in the midst of them."

CHAPTER TWENTY-THREE

GOD MEANT IT FOR GOOD

> But as for you, you meant evil against me; but God meant
> it for good. (Genesis 50:20)

J oseph addressed these words to his brothers after the death of their father, for they were filled with fear now that Joseph had them in his power, and they were awaiting punishment for the evil they had done.

They had been jealous of him and had hated him, and they even conspired in their hearts to kill him. And now, feeling their guilt, they awaited the judgment from their brother that they merited. But Joseph's response to their prayer, to their request for pardon, was: "Do not be afraid, for am I in the place of God?"

Joseph had to suffer greatly from the evil that his brothers had done, but he knew that it was not for him to judge them; there is only one judge: God. He also knew that whatever their intentions had been concerning him, God "had meant them for good."

THE WOUNDS OF A FRIEND

God sometimes blesses us in an unexpected manner, and quite often the trials and tribulations are a source of much greater blessing than we realise at that moment. David understood this well when he said: "It is good for me that I have been afflicted, that I may learn Your statutes" (Psalm 119:71).

It is not difficult to give thanks to God for his blessings when everything is going well in our life, when our brothers and our friends are kind to us, but it is difficult for us to do when we must suffer the wickedness and injustice of men.

Our friends become our enemies, and we become embittered and we pity ourselves. By this God tests our love and faithfulness to him.

Nothing is harder to withstand than the evil that is caused us by a brother or by someone whom we dearly love. The accumulated hatred in the hearts of Joseph's brothers caused them to sell him as a slave in Egypt, and the unjust accusation by his master's wife caused him to be placed in prison. He truly had enough reasons to be embittered! But the LORD was with Joseph; all these things were a source of blessings not only for Joseph and all his family, but also for Pharaoh and for all the Egyptian people who were saved from a terrible famine thanks to Joseph's visions and the power that God granted him.

THIS, TOO, IS FOR THE GOOD

Everything that happens to us can be used by God for our benefit and, if we accept everything by his hand, the evil that is done us as well as the good, we will have no place in our heart for bitterness, we will not pity ourselves, and we will not judge our enemies. On the contrary, we will be able to give thanks to God for our trials as well as for our joys. Paul wrote:

> All things work together for good to those who love God, to those who are the called according to His purpose. (Romans 8:28)

Paul not only gave thanks to God for his afflictions, but he glorified in them:

> And not only that, but we also glory in tribulations, knowing that tribulation produces perseverance; and perseverance, character; and character, hope. (Romans 5:3–4)

If we could also accept the evil that is done to us, we will be capable of loving our enemies, of blessing those who curse us, and of doing good to those who hate us. How could we hate those who do us evil if God changes everything for good? We do not want to curse them at all, but rather to bless them as Joseph blessed his brothers. Whereas, standing before him, they awaited judgment for all the evil that they had caused him, they received only words of love and blessing:

> "Now therefore, do not be afraid; I will provide for you and your little ones." And he comforted them and spoke kindly to them. (Genesis 50:21)

It is good that we should remember Joseph's example—of the evil that was caused him, and that God had meant it for good; but that which we must remember above all is his love, his certainty, his faith in God and his plans, his patience in the trials and tribulations, and the love that he showed his brothers in spite of the evil they had caused him.

EXCHANGING EVIL FOR GOOD

The shadows that surround us become darker each day and greatly seek to do us harm. Let us not fear them, let us not hate them, and let us not judge them. Let us give thanks to God for all these things; it is not enough to just thank him: let us glorify as Paul in the tribulations, being fully aware that God is with us. He instructs us and transforms even the most difficult trials for our benefit.

However, if we judge our enemies, if we allow bitterness to enter into our hearts, Satan can use us for his own plans. We will not be certain that God is with us unless we love our enemies as much as our friends. Love triumphs over evil; it is in blessing even those who conspire evil against us, if we learn that in doing so God can change the evil design against us into good, and those who conspired it can just as well become aware of the power and love of God. And in this way the evil that the enemy conspires in his heart can be meant for good.

.

CHAPTER TWENTY-FOUR

FAITH AND VISION

While we look not at the things which are seen, but at
the things which are not seen: for the things which are
seen are temporal; but the things which are not seen are
eternal. (2 Corinthians 4:18)

W e see with our physical as well as with our spiritual eyes.
Physical vision recognises only the facts of the world within
narrow confines. Spiritual vision knows no borders of matter, time,
or space. It penetrates into the spiritual realm and into eternity.

SPIRITUAL VISION

God gives his chosen ones spiritual vision, in order to reveal his
will and plan; in this way he led the fathers and the prophets,
and unveiled his plan of salvation and the way to its fulfilment.

Solomon said, "Without vision, the people perish;" Paul, "Without faith it is impossible to please God."

God gives a promise, a vision; however, if we do not have the
faith to wait for its fulfilment, we also perish. Perhaps we will have
to wait until the end of our lives; perhaps we will not experience
the fulfilment at all in this world; but through faith we know this:
God will truly accomplish all that he has promised and allowed
us to see.

SEEING THE PROMISE

As the children of Israel rested in the wilderness of Paran, the LORD spoke to Moses: "Send thou men, that they may search the land of Canaan, which I give unto the children of Israel: of every tribe of their fathers shall ye send a man, every one a ruler among them" (Numbers 13:3). The delegates were charged to reconnoitre the land, and ultimately to "see" what God had promised them.

Moses himself did not need to go with the twelve; in his inner vision, the promised land was already a reality to him.

THE REPORT

After forty days the scouts returned and made a report to the community of Israel about the land: "Indeed it flows with milk and honey." But they went on to say, "But the people who live in it are strong, and the cities are sturdy and large … they occupy the territory of the Negev … they live in the mountains … by the sea and on the bank of the Jordan." These were facts, which all twelve had seen. But ten of the scouts had only seen these things, and as they continued, "We could not move against this people; they are too strong for us. The land that we have traveled through … consumes its inhabitants, and the entire people that we saw there consists of nothing but giants," this caused fear and disappointment in the hearts of the people.

Two of them saw the situation in a different spirit, with different eyes, and said:

> Nevertheless, let us move out and conquer the land … If the LORD indeed wills, he will surely bring us into this land and give it to us … Only do not be insubordinate before the LORD, and fear not the people of this land; we will devour them. Their protection is gone from them, but the LORD is with us; do not be afraid of them.

THE TEN AND THE TWO

The ten saw the situation without inner vision or faith. Joshua and Caleb, on the other hand, saw the same situation with spiritual eyes and with faith, and therefore saw the victory of God according to his promise. What was impossible for men was yet possible with God, against whom the strongest enemy could not defend.

But the people were weak, and the "bad report" of the ten leaders stirred their hearts to such fear and rebellion that they did not want to listen to the two who were of a different mind. They attempted to stone them and to find another leader who would take them back to Egypt again.

RETRIBUTION

This enraged God to such an extent that only the prayers of Moses, Aaron, Joshua, and Caleb saved the people from extinction; however, as punishment, they were not allowed to enter the promised land. God said,

> Doubtless ye shall not come into the land, concerning which I sware to make you dwell therein, save Caleb ... and Joshua. But your little ones, ... them will I bring in, and they shall know the land which ye have despised. (Numbers 14:30–31)

RESPONSIBILITY

How great is the responsibility of the one whom God has called to oversee a community! They receive the greatest privileges, but much is required of them. They must have exemplary courage and faith, in order to strengthen the weak, in order to portray the vision vividly before the eyes of those who cannot see that far.

In Numbers 32:7–15 stands a warning for the tribes of Gad and Reuben, that they should not discourage the hearts of the children of Israel, as their fathers had done; otherwise, they would remain in the wilderness. "You will ruin this entire people."

A deficit of faith and vision in a leader can "ruin the entire people."

Many are called to leadership, but the only ones who are chosen are those whose faith does not waver, whose vision does not fade, who persevere to the end. Out of all the leaders of the tribes of Israel, only two were allowed to enter the promised land.

THE WAY INTO THE KINGDOM OF HEAVEN

Messiah has called many to be leaders for the wanderers in his kingdom. How many of them will be found to be faithful, to be called up by the King at his coming?

There are many difficulties on this path, many dangers, pitfalls, and struggles. But the land into which God is bringing us "is a very, very beautiful land." Numerous enemies attempt to weaken our faith and cause us to reverse course, but "their protection is gone from them, but the LORD is with us; do not be afraid of them."

Although our physical eyes perceive only the darkness around us, our spiritual eyes can see, as they are transformed into light. Therefore, we can pull through this darkness with steadfast certainty, because Messiah has said to us, "It has pleased your Father to give you the kingdom."

REALITY

When the Holy Spirit allows our inner eye to see the kingdom of Messiah, then this vision is reality to us, just as the promised land was for Moses. We do not need to "reconnoitre the land" to strengthen our faith, and when others, whose spiritual eyes are not open, seek to do so and to bring us a "bad report," we are not discouraged. When the entire people rebels and wishes to go back, we intercede for them, as Moses, Aaron, Joshua, and Caleb did.

Vision and faith lead us on the way to the kingdom; prayer, however, opens the eyes of the blind and saves the people from ruin.

CHAPTER TWENTY-FIVE

COMING HOME TO SOUTH AFRICA

After a twenty-eight-year absence I have returned to my home-land of South Africa. Geographically as well as spiritually, I have come a long way since I left the country, and it was clear to me that God brought me back for his purposes. I wait on his leading.

WALKING IN MIRACLES

I came to Cape Town on January 8, 1959, after a two-week journey by sea (9,000 km. from London), and marvelled at what lay before me. All I had with me in connection with our work was a small mailing list of readers of our periodicals in South Africa, who live dispersed within this large country. I asked myself how I could make connections with them, and which doors would open to me.

But God had organised everything beforehand, and during my two-and-a-half months in South Africa I walked in the way of miracles, on which God plans and orders everything to the last detail when the time is ripe for the gospel of the kingdom, and if we faithfully and patiently wait for him, he will take care of everything.

In this way it became possible for me to travel through all the provinces of the South African Union and to visit our readers in remote locations. This brought joy and encouragement to these lonely people who labour to show light and love to the Africans.

Our periodical is their only connection with Israel and their only source of news from that country, toward which their eyes and hearts are directed. They speak of our news as their "spiritual nourishment."

A SCANT FEW

There were only a few, a scant few, who had full understanding of the time in which we live, and who were fully aware of the coming kingdom, God's working in Israel, and the meaning of *JCG* [*Judenchristliche Gemeinde*, i.e., "Jewish Christian Community"]. Among them were two clergymen in the Dutch Reformed Church in South Africa, who have promulgated this message in their small communities for several years.

They stand alone; they are not understood by their colleagues, who wander on the same difficult paths as their brothers in other lands. However, they are chosen ones who know the way, and God used them to open the door for me to speak.

So gatherings were organised in Cape Town, Johannesburg, and Pretoria, and I was able to put forth our message in totally different circles: in churches, universities, and missionary societies; and among Messianic Jews and among Jews.

Many had heard nothing of our message or of the existence of a Messianic Jewish community. They were interested to hear about Israel, about how God has upheld the people and the land. This gave them an entirely new outlook.

To others the message was not new, but was received with doubt. Still others received light concerning their own problems and were deeply thankful that clarity had now replaced ambiguity.

But the few to whom God had already given our vision, those who had been waiting to come into personal contact with the Messianic Jewish community—they were so delighted. They were strengthened on their lonely path, and encouraged, and now feel consciously associated with the members of the brotherhood of the kingdom of Yeshua the Messiah in other countries.

The hand of God was clearly discernible on my entire trip in South Africa. The King has faithful subjects in every country; he has called them to unify themselves at this appointed hour, that warning and light might penetrate the surrounding darkness with greater strength.

CHAPTER TWENTY-SIX
THE RETURN

We are currently living in the age of the return of the Jewish people in the land of Israel. Theodore Herzl had a vision and the Zionist movement was created. Jews of all countries were passionate for this ideal of the return to Zion.

ZIONISM

The first pioneers sacrificed everything, often even their own lives, in response to this call. Others devoted their fortunes, their time, and their minds to it. Those who did not respond to the call of Zionism were forced to by other means: it was indeed the era set by God for the return of the Jewish people to their own country. But now, after thirteen years of the existence of the State of Israel, the flame of Zionism begins to dwindle; the light is fading.

The 25th World Zionist Congress was held this year in Jerusalem; it assembled delegates from almost all the countries of the world. This congress noted the current weakness of Zionism and the confusion that reigns at the heart of the movement. After the great success that it knew at its inception, Zionism must currently fight and search for new methods to carry out its plans, to revive the ideal of Zionism, and to rekindle the flame that flickers and goes out.

After two weeks of daily and nightly sessions, discussions and papers, the congress had to realise that they had found no new force of impetus, no clarity as to the path that Zionism must now take. In its initial call, Zionism invited Jews to return to the land of their fathers. It now invites them to return to the Hebrew language and the Jewish education system, in Israel as well as in the Diaspora. The danger is now quite great that Jews who live in other countries will lose their identity as Jews.

THE JOURNEY OF RETURN

Zionism was an instrument that guided the first steps of the Jewish people in their journey of return. The work of this movement was blessed, for this call to return was God addressing his people Israel. But the journey of return is long and we are only at the beginning of the road. The Jewish people are returning to their country. It is also their return to national independence, to their language, to the synagogue, and also to the Bible—consecutive stages of the journey. Zionism's flame glows in these different stages; nevertheless, these cannot be the end goal for those who return to the land. The journey of the return of Israel does not end at Zion—the Jews must go further. "If you desire to return, O Israel—return to Me," says the LORD.

The final goal is not the State, but the Kingdom of Israel, where the Messiah will meet all those who continued on the journey to the very end. But at the current stage in the journey, where there is no clearly defined vision of the final destination, Satan intervenes and "changes the tracks." He leads the blind down a dead-end street, he lays traps for the disobedient, he leads the insane astray, and encourages the proud to follow their own path, far from the way marked out and prepared by God.

It was the same in the days of the Prophet Hosea. "They return," he said, "but it is not to the Most High that they return" (Hosea 7:16). They return to the land, but not to heaven. They cry out to the LORD, but "they do not cry to Me in their hearts. They gather together to obtain wheat and barley, but they distance themselves from Me." They seek to build and defend themselves using the model of other countries, and they serve their gods as they did in the past, forgetting the power and the commandments of the God of Israel.

THE BIBLE

Of all the stages in this journey of return, it is at the stage of the return to the Bible that Satan intervenes with the most cunning; it is there that the danger is greatest. We find that Bible study groups of all sorts have been started by the President and the Prime Minister—biblical courses, Bible trivia, and daily biblical lectures on the radio. The Bible is becoming a point of interest and attraction in Israel. But this return to the Bible is not a return to God—it is only a stage of the journey.

Plenty of divergent spirits are inspiring these biblical encounters. Some groups are connected only with the talmudic tradition, while the dominant theme of others is that of intellect, pride, or knowledge. One can understand the Bible only in accordance with the measure of the spirit that one possesses. Mr. Ben-Gurion recently praised King Saul during his Bible study group meeting and called him the most "perfect king without faults" in the history of Israel. He described him as being "a great hero—and a modest king," and accused David of injustice, disloyalty, declaring that he has been wrongfully praised all throughout the history of Israel.

The "heroism and modesty" of King Saul, as Ben-Gurion attributes to him, is typical of present day Israel. The humility of King David can be comprehended only by an Israel that has a humble heart. In this return of Israel to the Bible, Satan uses all human failings and blindness to prevent them from "returning to the Most High." However, there are also Bible study groups in Israel where the Bible is taught by the light of the Messiah, where the true vision of return is recognised and understood.

The Bible is the light that guides the final steps of the travellers, and in spite of all of Satan's efforts to distort this light, he can neither prevent nor delay the divine plan. The power of the shadows is very strong in Israel, most of all in Jerusalem, but within all these shadows there is always a ray of light, the light that guides our final steps on the path of return.

REPENTANCE

It is God who gave the Hebrew language to his people, and each word has a profound meaning. The Hebrew word for "return" is "*shuvah*,"[19] which means "repentance." The return is a repentance. There cannot be a true return of the Jewish people without repentance. Until Israel comprehends this, until the heart of the Jews is transformed and humble before God, they will wander aimlessly on all paths, avoiding the only path that brings their journey of return to an end.

We hear these words from the Prophet Amos:

> You were as a firebrand plucked out of the furnace. In spite of this, you have not returned to me, said the LORD … prepare to meet your God, O Israel! (Amos 4:11–12)

And Ezekiel adds:

> Just as I entered into judgment with your fathers in the desert of the land of Egypt, so too will I enter into judgment with you, says the Lord GOD. I will cause you to pass under the rod … I will separate the rebels from you … and a remnant will return to the LORD. (Ezekiel 20:36–38; Isaiah 10:22)

SUDDENLY

All the events of Israel's history are planned and foreseen by God; they will come at the moment set by him. Many events seem to occur "suddenly" in Israel—but in reality they have been planned for many years. When King Hezekiah purified the Temple and re-established the true religion after the idolatrous reign of King

---

[19] [*Shuvah* is actually the first person command form, whereas *teshuvah* is the noun form.]

Ahaz, "when all was put back in order and the service of the House of the LORD was re-established," we read that "Hezekiah and the entire people rejoiced that God had prepared the people, for the thing was done *suddenly*" (2 Chronicles 29:35–36).

God planned the re-establishment of the State of Israel, which seemed to occur suddenly. God is currently planning the establishment of the Kingdom of Israel, and the King will return "suddenly" to establish his kingdom, "planned since before the foundation of the world."

THE FINAL STEPS

We are en route toward the kingdom; we are approaching the final stages of the journey of return—we are arriving at the age where Israel must "pass under the rod," where the LORD "will separate from Israel the rebels and the unfaithful." The fading of the light of Zionism shows us just how near we are to the time when a new light will shine in Israel, the light that announces the return of Messiah Yeshua, the King of the Jews. Only those Jews who possess the light of Messiah and the vision of his return in their hearts can make this luminous signal known. We believe that God is currently preparing his witnesses in Israel, and at the appointed time their voices will be heard. Everything is prepared in the plan of God, but *it will arrive suddenly, at the appointed time.* The State of Israel is presently following the model of Saul's kingdom; this is confirmed by the admiration for Saul that is expressed by the current leader of Israel. God will reject the State of Israel in the same manner that he rejected the kingdom of Saul for his disobedience to the divine commandments. But the kingdom of David succeeded that of Saul's, and the Messiah will reign upon the throne of David. Israel is going to reach the goal of its journey of return: the kingdom of Israel.

Return to Me and I will return to you, says the LORD.

CHAPTER TWENTY-SEVEN

TO OBEY IS BETTER THAN SACRIFICE

When God chooses for himself a servant to accomplish a special mission, he equips him with everything that he will need to successfully complete that task. However, he requires two things of the one he has elected: obedience and humility.

As we study the character of the first two kings of Israel, Saul and David, we are presented with a very significant image by which we may understand the importance of this obedience and humility required by God.

Saul, once he learned from Samuel that he had been chosen to be king of Israel, responded: "Am not I a Benjamite, of the smallest of the tribes of Israel? And my family the least of all the families of the tribe of Benjamin? Wherefore then speakest thou so to me?" (1 Samuel 9:21). He was therefore driven by a spirit of humility that is pleasing to God, conscious of his own insignificance—and Samuel received the command to anoint him king of Israel. Yet Samuel declared to the people: "See ye him whom the LORD hath chosen, that there is none like him among all the people?" (1 Samuel 10:24).

This is how Saul's reign in Israel began. Samuel was the spokesman of the LORD; he gave him his instructions and assigned him the task of liberating Israel from the yoke of the Philistines and of leading Israel in the ways of God.

THE TEST

Saul received his first orders from the mouth of Samuel: he must go to Gilgal and await Samuel for seven days; Samuel would offer burnt offerings and sacrifices of peace offerings, and would tell him what he must do (1 Samuel 10:8).

How did Saul, the king, obey these orders? It is written that he did not await Samuel, but that after seven days he himself offered the burnt offering. When Samuel arrived immediately thereafter and he told him that he had "acted foolishly" in disregarding the order of the LORD, Saul justified himself by declaring to Samuel that he had indeed obeyed that order and waited for seven days, but that Samuel did not come and the people were scattering far from him. He was afraid that the Philistines would attack some of them. That is why he felt forced to offer the burnt offering (I Samuel 13:8–14).

HOWEVER …

In Saul's response to his first test of obedience and submission his entire character is thereby found revealed: weakness in his faith, pride, and an inability to submit his human reasoning humbly to God. His character traits appear throughout his entire life in each subsequent test and they cause him to lose the throne. Yet, in spite of Samuel's words after his first disobedience ("But now thy kingdom shall not continue … because thou hast not kept that which the LORD commanded thee"), Saul still had other occasions during his reign to repent and to triumph over his weaknesses. However, he did not take advantage of them.

A little while later Saul received this order: "Strike Amalek, and utterly destroy everything that belongs to him; you shall not spare him!"

Once again Saul disobeyed; he could not execute this order in its *entirety*. And once again he justified himself to Samuel: "Yea, I have obeyed the voice of the LORD, and have gone the way which the LORD sent me, and have brought Agag the king of Amalek, and have utterly destroyed the Amalekites. But the people took of the spoil, sheep and oxen, the chief of the things which should have been utterly destroyed, to sacrifice unto the LORD thy God in Gilgal" (1 Samuel 15:20–21).

REJECTION

When God gives us an order, he requires us to obey him to the smallest details and to the very end. He has no need of our advice, nor of any modification that we might suggest from the "wisdom" of our human thought. His decisions may appear illogical to us, for the ways of God are not our ways, and it is only in humility and total obedience that we can execute the orders received from God. To be his servants, he requires obedience and submission of us.

Saul obeyed the first part of the instructions he received. He waited for seven days at Gilgal, but he could not wait until the very last minute of the seventh day—he could not wait until Samuel's arrival. His faith left, fear overcame him, and he followed the suggestions of his human reasoning in lieu of humbly awaiting the divine intervention. He obeyed up until the last moment, but his inability to resist *in the last moment* the suggestions of his reasoning cancelled out his obedience for those seven days.

During the war with the Amalekites he showed the same weakness. He obeyed all the orders except the last. Once again, he attempted to improve the orders of God; he wanted to save the life of King Agag, and the voice of the people influenced him just as during his first test. "But the people took of the spoil, sheep and oxen, the chief of the things which should have been utterly destroyed, to sacrifice unto the LORD thy God." And Samuel responded with these words of the LORD: "Behold, to obey is better than sacrifice, and to hearken than the fat of rams."

After this second disobedience, Saul lost his kingship: "For thou hast rejected the word of the LORD, and the LORD hath rejected thee from being king over Israel … The LORD hath rent the kingdom of Israel from thee this day, and hath given it to a neighbour of thine, that is better than thou" (1 Samuel 15:26–28).

Saul then understood his error and confessed: "I have sinned: for I have transgressed the commandment of the LORD, and thy words: because I feared the people, and obeyed their voice" (I Samuel 15:24).

However, Saul did not accept his rejection with real humility, thus he pleaded to Samuel: "Yet honour me now, I pray thee, before the elders of my people, and before Israel" (1 Samuel 15:30).

Saul lost his kingship by his disobedience. He could not humble himself neither before God nor before men. Although he knew his sin, he could not present to God a heart truly prepared for repentance and accept his defeat. His pride prevented him from humbling himself, even though he recognised his sin, and this is why "the Spirit of the LORD departed from Saul" (1 Samuel 16:14).

THE SUCCESSOR

We then read in the history of the two kings that the Spirit of the LORD rested upon David, who was anointed king and successor of Saul. "God chose for himself a man after his own heart."

While David was still but an adolescent, he opposed the enemy of Israel; this was his first test of faith. He was determined to fight against Goliath, the strongest Philistine, not with sword or spear, but with his words: "Thou comest to me with a sword, and with a spear, and with a shield: but I come to thee in the name of the LORD of hosts, the God of the armies of Israel, whom thou hast defied … for the battle is the LORD's, and He will give you into our hands" (1 Samuel 17:45–47).

How different this attitude and this faith are from those of Saul! How much more so did David have the right to say "but …" when he found himself before an enemy such as Goliath! David's faith was firm and he was obedient to the LORD. And what was his reaction when, after having disobeyed the orders of the LORD, he was confronted with his sin? When Nathan made him realise his sin against Uriah, David was seized with fear and was immediately ready to accept his punishment from the hand of God with a humble and repentant heart. And when Shimei pronounced curses against David, he responded: "So let him curse, because the LORD hath said unto him, Curse David. Who shall then say, Wherefore hast thou done so?" (2 Samuel 16:10). When his son Absalom became his enemy, he did not fight him at all, and he gave his soldiers orders not to wound him. And he wept over him bitterly until he learned of his death.

Quite the opposite, Saul could not endure any form of punishment by the hand of God. From the moment when David's renown surpassed his own, he sought to kill him. His pride could not endure the praises that David received, this young man, for having killed his ten thousand, since he himself had killed only one thousand. He pursued him like his worst enemy because he knew that the LORD had chosen him to be his successor.

Nevertheless David continued to venerate in Saul the anointing of the LORD, and when he was delivered into his hands he did not desire to do any harm to him and spared his life. Once Saul was finally killed, David wept and mourned the fate of this powerful man.

PRIDE

David was humble, and in his humility he was always prepared to listen to God and accept everything that came from his hand, successes and humiliations alike. But Saul, in his pride and jealousy, did not know how to humble himself before God.

When Saul entered the hands of David, and when he exercised mercy toward him, Saul understood just how foolishly he had acted: "I have sinned: return, my son David: for I will no more do thee harm, because my soul was precious in thine eyes this day: behold, I have played the fool, and have erred exceedingly" (1 Samuel 26:21). "And David said in his heart, I shall now perish one day by the hand of Saul," (1 Samuel 27:1) and he took refuge in the land of the Philistines in order to escape him.

David venerated Saul, but he could not confide in him for he had learned well to recognise the spirit that compelled Saul. Saul frequently recognised his sin; however, it was not enough to recognise his sin, he still needed to possess in his heart a true feeling of repentance. When grace is given us to recognise our transgressions, if we persist in our errors, we are refusing to learn that which God wants us to learn, and his spirit turns away from us.

SUBMISSION

The examples taken from the lives of Saul and David can be a source of enrichment for us, and they allow us to understand the will of God when he requires obedience and submission of us. Perhaps we believe ourselves to be obedient just as Saul believed. It is a very common mistake to want to explain away and disregard the divine orders that we have not executed because of the arguments coming from our own reasoning. Doubt and questioning things that our reasoning cannot understand can prevent us from completing our task in its entirety with complete faith.

Since Samuel was a long time in coming, Saul believed it wiser to take action himself than to wait. He was aware of his importance as king. But David remained fearless before the enemy. He did not ask himself if it was rational, sensible, or even possible to march against Goliath without a sword or spear, and he refused the helmet and armour that Saul made him carry. He only had a slingshot and a few stones. He knew only one thing: this enemy had defied the God of Israel, therefore the battle is in the hands of God. He marched against the enemy and killed him, completely submitted to God and full of faith in his power.

The divine orders must be executed in total obedience, with a submission that knows neither fear nor doubt, that rejects all pride and all human reasoning, and that knows no other justification except the will of God. We can then be certain that the Spirit of God abides with us.

TOTAL OBEDIENCE

Saul was unrepentant; he only obeyed partially. David was obedient and submissive; nevertheless his human weakness caused him to deviate from the path of obedience. His sincere repentance saved his kingship and prepared the way for the One who is greater than he and who would finally reign over Israel.

Yeshua came a first time in Israel to show, through his life, that which is *total obedience and true submission*. He came down in human form and was subject to all the same temptations as we are. He was obedient, humble, and submissive before God even until death—his death on the cross.

When God calls us, once he gives us a task to accomplish, are we capable of walking in his footsteps on the path of obedience and submission, and of following that path to the very end, until the very last minute, until death if necessary?

The last step is the most important. If Yeshua had lived all his life in obedience only to shy away at the last moment, the world would not yet be saved today.

If we must be obedient and submissive all our lives, let us especially ask God for the grace to remain obedient and submissive until the last hour, until the last minute. Let us follow Yeshua until *the last minute*, until the cross. From there we will then be able to follow him on the Eternal Way as well.

CHAPTER TWENTY-EIGHT

IN YOU SHALL ALL THE FAMILIES OF THE EARTH BE BLESSED

Dear friends, when we examine the future, it is with faith in the complete and precise fulfilment of all the promises of God. If, on the other hand, we cast a glance on the past, it is to understand that many of these promises have already been fulfilled and to review our present situation.

JEWS IN ENGLAND

This year, in England, the Jews reflect on what happened three hundred years ago; they celebrate the third century of their re-establishment in England, in Great Britain. The first time they came to England was in 1066, and they remained under the protection of the kings until Edward I in 1290, who decreed that the Jews must be expelled from the country. Thus for 365 years no Jews were to be found in England. The year 1656 was extremely important for the history of the Jews, the history of England, and the history of the world, because this readmission of Jews in England was, at the same time, the first step for their readmission and return to the Holy Land, to Palestine.

It was in that year that two inspired men sought to bring the Jews back to England. One of these was Menasseh ben Israel, a prominent rabbi in the Jewish community of Amsterdam. The other was Oliver Cromwell, the great man and protector of England during the Commonwealth. Menasseh ben Israel sent a petition to Oliver Cromwell, requesting from him the readmission and resettlement of the Jews in England. And despite the opposition of his compatriots, this petition was granted, although Cromwell had known from experience what this represented economically and politically. There was another motive at the root of the decision of these two great men: both of them knew and had the vision that we have today, the vision of the Millennial Kingdom. They both believed that the coming of the Messiah was imminent. Cromwell indeed awaited the return of Christ, and Menasseh ben Israel equally awaited the coming of the Messiah. So that was the common factor, the common motive, that caused Menasseh ben Israel and Cromwell to act for the resettlement of the Jews in England.

Because Cromwell believed in the imminent return of Christ, he believed that for this reason it was a Christian's duty to help the Jews, to accept them and recognise them. Menasseh ben Israel believed that when the dispersion of the Jews was fulfilled and finished, the Messiah would come. He knew and possessed evidence that the Jews were dispersed in all the earth, and that they still must be dispersed in England. And so in 1656 the Jews were once again permitted to enter into England. Thus throughout these past three centuries, England has constituted a notable refuge for the persecuted Jews fleeing from many European countries.

FROM OUT OF LONDON

And the presence of Jews in England was an equally great advantage for this country; not only did they enrich their country in all aspects of life—in the economic realm, the political, and others—but the blessing of the Most High rested on the country. This is why England prospered and the British Empire obtained power, for the LORD had said to Israel: "I will bless those who bless you." England had a mission to accomplish as regarding the Jews, which began to be manifest in 1621 through the publication of a book on the restoration of the Jews. The fact that the English love their Bible and believe in the prophecies awakened in them a boundless sympathy for the Jews.

The first proposals for the creation of Jewish colonies in Palestine began in the nineteenth century, and from then on we see many famous names in connection with the desire to re-establish the Jews in their own country. Theodore Herzl himself said: "From the moment that I entered into this movement, my eyes turned toward England." It is in England that Herzl had his first Zionist conference and published his first Zionist article. During the first Zionist congress in Basle, England was represented by eight delegates. It was in England that Chaim Weizmann arrived, and the result of his first contact with Lord Balfour is well known, since the Balfour Declaration gave a national home to the Jews in the Holy Land under the mandate of Great Britain. And with the opening of a home for the Jews in Palestine came the arrival of Jews from all parts of the world to this country. It was in this way that the foundation upon which the State of Israel was built was laid. Thus, when we reflect back three hundred years, we see the importance of Great Britain's message; not only did Zionism prosper and such men as Herzl and Weizmann find sympathy and understanding, but also the first Messianic Jewish communities were birthed in the Holy Land.

Their members came from different countries: from South Africa, Austria, and Germany to meet primarily in England. It was in London that the first Messianic Jewish conferences took place, which were met with sympathy and aid from the Gentile Christians of all nations.

The first prayer meetings amongst Jewish and Gentile Christians occurred in London, and it opened the door and the way to understanding for these two people groups throughout the entire world, and there were Jews who made this long voyage, for their fate was through England.

THE NEXT STAGE

And now where are we going? Cromwell believed that England had a mission to accomplish in regard to the Jews. He was right. It was indeed the mission of England to help them return to their land in order to prepare themselves and gather together for the return of the Messiah. Menasseh ben Israel, from his part, believed that the dispersion of the Jews in all the earth had to be fulfilled before the Messiah returned. He was also right. The Jews had to pass through England before being regathered from all the countries to return to their homeland. Now we have seen the fulfilment of all these things. The Jews have indeed been dispersed in all the countries of the earth. They were later assembled in their own land where their State was created. And we also have before our very eyes the beginning of the conversion of Jews in Israel, their conversion to Messiah. There are Jews who belong to the nation of Israel who consider Yeshua to be the Messiah and they await his coming. What will be the following stage? Our attention is now directed to Jerusalem, which is the political and spiritual centre of Israel. It is there that all the nations will come in judgment. Yeshua told his disciples that in the last times one nation will arise against another and, he adds, "You will see Jerusalem surrounded by armies." This is what we see today. With the appearance of the Messianic Jewish community, the vanguard of the Jewish nation that carries the royal banner—that is, the cross within the Star of David, which proclaims the approach and return of the King—the end of the road is already in view. It is for this reason that the royal banner must remain raised in Jerusalem. It will enter into the kingdom through the vicissitudes it endures while Jerusalem will be surrounded by armies. The Lord will sound out his voice from Jerusalem, the spirit of grace will be spread upon the inhabitants of Jerusalem, and you will see in Jerusalem a city of rest. In our days Jews and Gentiles walk together, having in their charge the Jewish banner and saluting the King who is returning.

As long as this banner waves in any country, that country will receive a blessing and will be illuminated by the light of the

Most High. From now on Israel will not have to search for help amongst the nations, for God himself will manifest his power amongst them. When the Messiah will come, the conversion of Israel will be accomplished. Then its mission amongst the nations will begin, for the LORD said to Abraham: "In you shall all the families of the earth be blessed."

CHAPTER TWENTY-NINE
A WORLDWIDE MOVEMENT

D uring my first encounter with some members of the Messianic Jewish movement, after having received the certainty that we share the same faith, they asked me to join them and labour with them in a worldwide movement. At this time, the "worldwide movement" was a small group of four Messianic Jews reunited in London, a movement that seemed quite humble and insignificant. I confess that this term "worldwide movement" took me a bit by surprise. But all that I desired was to serve my Messiah whom I had just found.

I still did not possess a sufficiently developed prophetic sense to be able to see so far ahead. I was at the school of "the children of the prophet,"[20] and I wanted to walk in the faith as the "children of the prophet" walked with Elijah.

Soon I was already being used as an instrument and I was able to learn through experience that this Messianic Jewish community in London, so insignificant at the beginning, must truly become a worldwide movement through which the message and the call must spread across all the countries of the world. My first steps brought me to Israel, where we established a small citadel; and we have now held this fortress for fourteen years, keeping the banner of the kingdom waving, awaiting the marching order of our King.

---

[20] [Ref. 2 Kings 2:3 (בני הנביאים). Also translated as "the company of the prophets" or "the disciples of the prophets."]

Since then, my task, which was equally that of the other members of the Community, was to proclaim the message of the kingdom in many countries, from Scandinavia to South Africa to Australia.

Such are the ways of God. He gives his prophet eyes that allow him to see the realities of the future. Elijah *heard* the rain long before his servant was even able to perceive a small cloud. When God gives us a vision, it is already a reality.

THE COMMUNITY IN ISRAEL

However, Israel is the centre of our work. Our call was to prepare the way of the kingdom of Israel. Jerusalem, the city where the "thrones of judgment" will be erected, the city where the Messiah lived and to where he shall return—we had to conquer it. It was not an easy task. If our beginnings in London were small and insignificant, in Israel they were smaller still and seemingly even more insignificant.

It has been fourteen years now since we lit the lights of the Messiah on the Mount of Olives for the first time. Afterward, the small community that formed around this light had to undergo plenty of attacks and was almost broken, but nothing was able to destroy it. What followed were the trials of the war and the siege, the sufferings of hunger and thirst, the constant dangers of an uninterrupted rain of fragments and bullets fired by the enemy, and being held in custody as spies with the threat of being shot. These were the beginnings of the community in Israel.

From a human point of view, this small community of half a dozen members, all of them weak, despised, and fearful, could never in any way be considered as the centre of a worldwide movement. How ridiculous this all was! How long would it remain under such conditions? What significance could it have in Israel? The battles for the formation of the State were underway; Israel's independence was being defended. The world could see these victories, and all were amazed over the miracles that made the birth of the State of Israel possible.

But what about the Messianic Jewish Community in Israel? The centre of the worldwide movement! The power that controls it, the "Rock" upon which it was founded, no one could see. And of its victories, only those who had received the grace to see the vision of the kingdom and to know the Leader of this Community could see them.

PROTECTION OF THE MESSIAH

Throughout all these years, the Community was constantly the prey of spiritual attacks. It increased and decreased in number, the light moved from place to place, but even though it was the target of spiritual attacks, it was also placed under the protection of the Messiah.

I lit the lights of the Messiah for the first time on the Mount of Olives during my first visit to Palestine in 1946. I shared in all the sufferings of the birthing of the State of Israel during my second stay in Palestine. And during my numerous subsequent visits I shared in all the trials, difficulties, vicissitudes, and attacks that the Community had to suffer. I am currently in Israel again, and when I consider the past years, I see with wonder and thanksgiving how the hand of God has always protected and blessed this work!

The light now shines radiantly in its sanctuary. All the strange spirits were eliminated; the faithful souls were strengthened. The citadel was maintained; the enemy was kept in check.

In the course of the last twelve years, the message has gone around the world, gathering other people who share this vision; during this time, in Jerusalem, the meeting centre saw its spiritual power increase and deepen. We believe that the time has now come to take a new step forward in this country. The way has been prepared.

THE MEASURE OF SUCCESS

This "worldwide movement," which began through the vision that Abram Poljak had, is still neither known nor recognised by the world. Its successes cannot be measured according to human criteria; its ways are difficult, its members few in number, its message is ridiculed or combatted. How can it withstand its enemies? How can its voice be heard among the tumult of the voices of this world?

Its successes are measured by the power of the spirit; one can see whether or not it is governed by love. The difficulties and the trials on its path are proof that it follows Yeshua, the Messiah. Did he not actually say: "If any man will come after me, let him deny himself, and take up his cross, and follow me" (Matthew 16:24)? Its members are few in number—they were as well when Messiah was on the earth: He chose only twelve disciples to continue his work. Its message is ridiculed and combatted just as Yeshua's message was by the Pharisees of that era. But it can withstand the most powerful enemies, for it is like "a house built on the rock." Its voice will rise above the tumult of human voices because it proclaims the Word of God and because "the heavens and earth will pass away, but My words shall not pass away," says the LORD.

All those who follow this way know only one leader: Yeshua the Messiah; to him be the praise, honour, and glory! Today, only the sheep of his flock hear his voice, but he has declared: "And other sheep I have, which are not of this fold: them also I must bring, and they shall hear my voice; and there shall be one fold, and one shepherd" (John 10:16). Such is the vision that we have of the Messianic Kingdom on earth—"one fold, and one shepherd"—a worldwide movement! May we have the grace to keep our eyes fixed on this One Shepherd; may we hear his voice above all the voices of this present world.

From the beginning, this was a long march on a battlefield, and we have not yet reached the end. We must fight greater battles; but the victory is certain, the final victory, the conquest of the satanic authority over this earth—during the return of the Messiah. Then the Kingdom of Israel will be recognised and acclaimed throughout the world—the Messianic Kingdom of peace on earth.

THE UNITED NATIONS

There is a worldwide movement that is recognised today by all the peoples of the earth, acclaimed by all, and toward which all the countries turn to find a solution to the world's problems. Its centre is in New York: it is called the "United Nations."

As we write these words, the leaders of all countries meet in this centre to strive to find out how to establish peace on earth. Security, unity, justice for all the inhabitants of the earth: these are its goals.

It is in a large, impressive building in the city that is the heart of modern civilisation, in magnificent conference rooms in which the leading members of the "United Nations" meet. It is there that they discuss peace, but the illusions made by nice sounding words and disguised sentiments are so thin that they have difficulty hiding the latent conflicts amongst the peoples, the hatred, and the thirst for power that they must conceal.

It was right to choose New York as the centre of this movement; it is a city that symbolises the human pride of success, material riches, and power. One can see people's efforts to resolve the world's problems by means of their own strength and pride.

There they incessantly discuss the rights and demands of the people; each one proposes his own solution to resolve these problems; each one has his own ideas on the means by which to obtain peace. It is there that we find the forces that proclaim "peace, peace, when there is no peace." They ignore or reject God, and when God is not at the centre, Satan has free reign.

Such is the worldwide movement that the countries of the world have accepted as the instrument of peace.

OASES OF LIGHT

How different it is, this worldwide movement that looks only to God to find the solution to all problems, and can conceive of peace only by means of the kingdom of God on earth, under the direction of the Messiah! Its centre could never be established in

New York, for "the law shall go forth of Zion, and the word of the LORD from Jerusalem" (Micah 4:2).

Although the centre of this worldwide movement in Jerusalem may still be very small today, unknown by the peoples, the power of its light and the spiritual stream of its blessings for the nations have already been revealed to those whose minds God has enlightened.

The countries that responded to the call of Jerusalem saw centres, emanating from this movement, established in their territory and they have already received spiritual blessings from them. There are currently three of these oases of light, preparing the way of the kingdom, in France, Germany, and Switzerland. These are places of repose, peace, and recovery, where one may study the Bible with a new perspective, where one may proclaim the message of the kingdom, and where one may search the path of life of this kingdom.

There is one law that governs life in these centres, one law by which all problems may be resolved, whether it be on an individual or national level—it is the law of love. It is one law that cannot be observed without a complete change of each person's heart. Only the Messiah has the ability to direct the heart of men in this sense.

Men, women, and children come into these centres from many countries, guided by one spirit alone, sharing one same vision, looking to the same leader. All the barriers of nationalities, languages, cultures, and personalities fall, and we truly see the "United Nations" in the true sense of the term—a token of what is to come when the kingdom of God will be established and all people will be subject to the law of the Messiah.

It is not the powerful men of this world that come into these centres of light and union, but the poor, weak, and the despised. God cannot work through prideful hearts—it is with gentle people of humble heart that he can build his kingdom and demonstrate the power of his Spirit.

CENTRED IN JERUSALEM

This community that is so small, which carries the banner of the worldwide movement of the kingdom in its centre in Jerusalem, will remain small; the world will not accept it before the reappearance of its Leader; but it will receive greater spiritual powers still. With humility of heart and in repentance, Israel and the nations will recognise it only when the Messiah returns and manifests all his power on earth; only then will people understand that he alone can unite the nations and bring peace on earth.

The small streams of blessings that today spread over the nations will then become rushing torrents covering the whole earth; everything that was built by the hands of men on human foundations will collapse and be carried away by the floods of the redemption.

We search for the strength, power, and peace from the source, beside him in whose honour we light and carry the flame in Jerusalem, and we patiently await the day when all the peoples and all the creatures of the earth shall worship God and when "the inhabitants of the earth shall learn justice."

> Many nations shall come and say: Come, and let us go up to the mountain of the LORD ... and he will teach us of his ways, and we will walk in his paths. For the law shall go forth of Zion, and the word of the LORD from Jerusalem. And he shall judge among many peoples, and rebuke strong nations far off. They shall beat their swords into plowshares, and their spears into pruning hooks; nation shall not lift up a sword against nation, neither shall they learn war any more. But they shall sit every man under his vine and under his fig tree; and none shall make them afraid; for the mouth of the LORD of hosts hath spoken it. (Micah 4:2–4)

It is the mouth of the LORD of hosts that has spoken!

CHAPTER THIRTY
LADY OF MOUNT ZION

*Excerpts from Evie Garratt BBC Radio interview segment titled
"Ha-Ohel" for "Home this Afternoon," BBC Radio 4, August 13, 1969.*

In her 1969 BBC radio interview with Pauline Rose, Evie Garratt
described a visit to Pauline Rose's home, "Ha-Ohel," on Mount
Zion. She described the ascent up the winding road that climbed
"a hill of scrub and stone and derelict buildings" on its way to
the holy sites of Dormition Abbey and the Tomb of David. Before
reaching those destinations, Garratt came upon the home of Albert
and Pauline Rose, the only private home on Mount Zion, "A stone
house, in good order, with a luxurious garden."

In the interview, Pauline Rose explained why she and her
husband chose to live in such a dangerous spot, only a few yards
on the Israeli side of the Israeli-Jordanian border:

> PAULINE ROSE: I wanted to come here because I had the
> vision of Mount Zion and what it means. Mount Zion,
> we are told, is the place that God chose for his dwelling
> place, a place where the blessings would go out to all the
> world, a place where he would have his house of prayer,
> where all nations would flow into it. So, we felt that we
> would like to have a house on Mount Zion, which would
> be a place for all people to come. And, if God would help
> us, it would be a place of peace and joy and blessing.
> When I went to ask the authorities if we could come and

live here, they all were aghast and said "of course not, it's impossible. We can't have people living here because it is a holy sanctuary, and we can't have people living here because of the dangers. We wouldn't be responsible for anyone living here." But, I believe that what is impossible with man, is possible with God.

Pauline Rose went on to describe the red tape she and Albert encountered. At the time, she was in her early seventies and Albert was in his eighties. The government officials must have questioned the sanity of an elderly couple wanting to live in a war zone. Complicating the approval process was the uncertainty over which government office held jurisdiction over the abandoned homes on Mount Zion. After several years of negotiations and continued persistence, the Roses finally received permission to occupy a home on Mount Zion. They only needed to choose a house from a neighbourhood of homes left abandoned since the end of Israel's War of Independence in 1948:

> I saw this house which was right on the border and almost out of bounds and was in a very bad state of ruin because soldiers had been in here fighting in the War of Independence and then it was left like that for seventeen years. But, I felt this was the right house, right on the top of Mount Zion and with a wonderful view facing the Mount of Olives and the Kidron Valley, the Judean hills, and in the distance the mountains of Moab, and in between was the Dead Sea.

The house atop Mount Zion posed problems for the would-be renovators. Mount Zion could be accessed only by steep steps ascending from the Gihon side of the hill. The army used a military service road that came up the mountain, but the IDF restricted access. The Roses needed to obtain special permission to use the road:

> So we had another big fight to see if we could get the key of the barrier and be able to use this road. Otherwise, how

would we be able to restore this ruined building, bringing up building materials that would have to be brought up on a donkey's back up the steps? Finally, we won with the military and they gave us the key on the condition that it never passed out of our hands. When we tried the road, it was such a bad road that our car nearly went to pieces on its first journey. So we thought, well, we will have to have a jeep, same way as the soldiers. And just at that time, the Pope decided to come to Israel. So, this rough military road was turned into an asphalted road in a few weeks so that the Pope and his entourage could drive up to the top of Mount Zion. And I was very thankful to the Pope, because he made our coming here so much easier.

It took the Roses five months to complete their renovations before they could begin to move into their home on Mount Zion. In addition to the restoration of the abandoned house, Pauline wanted to plant a garden on Mount Zion. She believed that she had been called by God to plant a garden there as a prophetic sign of the promises about to be fulfilled:

> Another thing, which was in my vision, was a garden. In the Bible it says "make the place of my sanctuary beautiful." And I believe that Mount Zion was the place of God's sanctuary. So, I thought, if we can start by making a garden in order to beautify one small spot of Mount Zion that might later grow and the whole of Mount Zion would become a garden and beautiful. So we had to start removing the lorry loads of rubble, stones, and rubbish that had been here for hundreds of years and replacing it with loads of good soil and by building up the walls, the steps, the entrance to the house.

When Garratt visited the home in the fall of 1969, the garden had already been established for five years. She described a "beautiful garden where flowering plants grow in an amazing profusion and vines climb strongly up the walls and peach and plum and orange trees are heavy with fruit."

They hoped to make the home a place of hospitality for visitors, modelled after the exceptional hospitality of Abraham and Sarah. They even named the house on Mount Zion after Abraham's tent:

> We gave the house the name "Ha-Ohel," which is "The Tent," the name of Abraham's tent in the wilderness where all strangers were received with love and a welcome, and we hoped that the blessing that the people had in Abraham's tent would also come upon this house.

In 1964, the Roses began to receive visitors from all over the world. They hosted visitors from Europe who knew them from Pauline's work with Abram Poljak. They hosted visitors to Mount Zion who happened to see an occupied house and express curiosity. Evie Garratt said, "People of all creeds and from all walks of life, some to stay, some for a meal, some just passersby invited in for a cup of tea and a chat." The Roses kept visitor's guest books in which the visitors could leave messages. Many of the messages commented on the sense of spiritual peace and renewal the visitor felt in the presence of Ha-Ohel.

The Roses used their home to foster friendship and brotherly love between people from all walks of life. They maintained good relationships with all their neighbours: Jews, Arabs, and Christians. A dignified old Arab man on Mount Zion told Evie Garratt that Pauline Rose "is like a sister to me." The Jewish curator at the Holocaust Museum adjacent to the Rose home said, "She's an angel! An angel!" At the Franciscan Church, Father Benedict gladly inconvenienced himself to open the doors of his church to welcome Garratt and the Roses for a private tour, despite the lateness of the hour. He explained, "For the Roses, it is never after hours."

In June of 1968, the Six-Day War brought a temporary interruption to the spirit of calm and serenity that the Roses had fostered at Ha-Ohel. In the days leading up to the conflict, the IDF asked the Roses to leave for the sake of their own safety, but they refused:

We realised that it was a dangerous area and a battle zone, but we had no fears. So, we asked if we could remain here. We thought perhaps in some way we may be able to be of use. And, very reluctantly, they agreed. But, they would not allow us to stay in this house, because it was the most exposed place on Mount Zion. The Jordanian military posts were very near us, facing us and on either side of us. So they insisted that we go into a building at the back of our house which was a little safer.

Pauline Rose described the outbreak of the war on June 5:

The shells, the bullets, and the machine guns all started and I only had time to run into this building next door ... So, we had this battle, the soldiers were all around us firing from above us, on each side of us here on Mount Zion and the shells and the bullets coming from the other side. The noise was terrible and, really, it sounded as though the whole of Mount Zion would be destroyed.

During the course of the conflict, Pauline Rose made a tape recording of the sound of gunfire and explosions that surrounded her home. The BBC Radio interview played an audio clip of the recording. Rose commented, "The shelling and the battle continued without a stop until the morning of the seventh of June, and then it died down a little."

The Roses played a small part in the battle by housing IDF soldiers, offering them a place to briefly rest before their final push into the city. Pauline Rose had the privilege of hand-making an Israeli flag that those same IDF soldiers used to signal their conquest over the Old City:

At the same time, there were many new soldiers coming up to Mount Zion, they were very tired and weary as they hadn't had anything to drink or perhaps to eat for quite some time so we managed to make them some coffee before they went in. Before they had finished their coffee the commander of the unit came to me and said, "We are now going into the Old City from this side; our soldiers are also going in from the other parts and we have no flag, and we must have a flag with us, but we have no time to lose. What can you do to help us?" So I rushed upstairs and I pulled a sheet out of the cupboard and I happened to have a tube of blue paint and very quickly on the kitchen table we did the Magen David in this blue paint on the sheet, rushed downstairs, pulled a stick out of the garden to which we attached it, and they rolled it up and went down with their half-tracks and jeeps into the Old City through the border from Mount Zion. That was a great moment, and we wondered what would happen, and what would happen to that flag. Later, we learned that that was the flag that they put up on the tower of David when they conquered the city.